INTRO TO INVESTING

ROOPESH KANNAN

INDIA • SINGAPORE • MALAYSIA

CONTENTS

INTRODUCTION TO MONEY & FINANCE

Let's get one thing right – "MONEY MAKES THE WORLD GO ROUND."

Money has been a driving force behind human progress throughout history, shaping societies and economies and now, in the digital age, serving as the foundation of a complex and ever-changing financial system that affects every aspect of our lives.

Money's origins can be traced back to the dawn of human civilisation. In the absence of a standardised medium of exchange, societies relied on barter systems to trade goods and services.

Now let's understand the barter system and its flaws.

<u>WHAT IS BARTER?</u>

In an agrarian society with limited currency, the barter system emerges as a complex network of reciprocal exchanges. Consider a remote village with a well-known farmer and a skilled blacksmith. The blacksmith forges farming tools for the farmer, who in turn provides fresh produce to the blacksmith. This mutually beneficial arrangement exemplifies the essence of the barter system: a social fabric woven through interdependent exchanges in which parties recognise and value the unique contributions of each other. Without the use of money, this intricate dance of skill and provision exemplifies the barter system's reliance on mutual recognition and appreciation.

THE LIMITATIONS OF BARTER

The limitations of the barter system are obvious in modern economies. Finding suitable exchanges between people with different skills, assets, and needs is challenging, and often necessitates a "double coincidence of wants." Measuring the value of goods and services becomes difficult in the absence of a standardised unit of exchange, resulting in disagreements. Barter also stifles specialisation and growth by providing no means to store value or incentivise investments in specialised skills and complex manufacturing systems. Alternative monetary systems have emerged to address these complexities, facilitating trade, providing a common medium of exchange, and fostering economic development.

DEVELOPMENT OF COINS

The concept of cash extends back thousands of years to the earliest human civilisations. People wanted a medium of exchange to enable trade in ancient times. Cowrie shells were used as cash in the early days. Cowries were abundantly available and easily recognised, making them perfect for use as a unit of value. They were employed in many different locations of the world, from Africa to Asia, and even in portions of Europe. Cowrie shells were lightweight, portable, and durable, making them an ideal form of payment for small-scale transactions.

The necessity for a more standardised and convenient form of money became obvious as societies changed and trade increased. The introduction of coinage was the first notable breakthrough in this direction. The first recorded coins were introduced approximately 600

BCE in Lydia, an ancient country located in modern-day Turkey. These early coins were constructed of electrum, a naturally occurring gold-silver alloy. The Lydians standardised the weight and purity of their coins, creating a reliable medium of exchange that transformed commerce. The use of coinage spread fast throughout the ancient globe, with many civilisations minting their own coins and developing monetary systems.

Coins had several advantages over previous forms of currency. They provided a standardised unit of value, making transactions more efficient and reliable. Coins were portable, durable, and difficult to counterfeit, which added to their credibility. Coins facilitated long-distance trade because they were universally recognised and accepted. Different civilisations developed their own coinage systems, such as the Greeks, Romans, and Chinese, with intricate designs and symbols representing their culture and rulers.

The invention of coins not only changed economic transactions but also had profound cultural and political ramifications. Coins were frequently utilised to spread the influence of kings. Kings and emperors would have their names and images inscribed on coins to demonstrate their legitimacy and control over their respective territories. Coins were also important in documenting historical events and cultural landmarks. Today, they are valuable archaeological artefacts that shed light on ancient societies and provide insights into their economic, social, and political institutions. The invention of coinage was a watershed moment in human history, providing the groundwork for the intricate monetary systems that would emerge in the centuries that followed.

PAPER MONEY

The Tang Dynasty in 7th century China saw the first substantial development of paper money. Merchants and wealthy individuals would store their goods with trusted middlemen, who would provide a receipt as proof of deposit at the time. These receipts, dubbed "flying cash," could be traded for money, effectively functioning as an early form of paper currency. Paper money's convenience and efficiency were rapidly recognised, and the Chinese government began to formally produce banknotes.

The inherent limitations and challenges posed by coins contributed to the widespread adoption of paper money. Carrying huge amounts of currency became cumbersome and inconvenient as trade developed. Furthermore, coins were prone to wear, forgery, and debasement, all of which reduced their value and reliability. Paper money introduced a lightweight and easily divisible alternative, making transactions more practical and efficient.

Paper money's use grew outside China over time, reaching other parts of the world. Private banknotes printed by financial entities first appeared in Europe around the 17th century. These banknotes were initially backed by gold or silver deposits held by the issuing bank. They made payment more convenient and helped to solve the problems connected with moving and storing actual money.

IMPORTANCE OF FINANCIAL LITERACY

It refers to the knowledge, skills, and understanding needed to make informed and effective financial, personal finance, and investment decisions. Here are a few key reasons why financial literacy is important:

1. Individuals who are financially literate are better able to manage their personal finances. It enables them to make budgets, track expenses, save money, and make educated borrowing, investing, and retirement planning decisions. Individuals who are financially literate are better equipped to achieve their financial goals and build long-term wealth.
2. Individuals who are financially literate contribute to a country's overall economic stability and growth. They are more likely to make responsible financial decisions, reducing their reliance on government assistance and the strain on public resources.

Individuals who are financially empowered can make informed decisions about job choices, entrepreneurship, and investment opportunities, resulting in economic growth and prosperity.

3. It teaches people about the consequences of excessive debt and high-interest borrowing. It teaches them how to manage credit wisely, avoid predatory lending practices, and make informed loan and mortgage decisions. People can avoid financial distress and maintain a healthy financial life by understanding the fundamentals of interest rates, debt management, credit scores, etc.

4. Personal finance is a constantly changing field. Individuals who are financially literate are better prepared than most to navigate the ever-evolving landscape of financial products, digital payments, cryptocurrencies, and emerging technologies. It prepares us to adapt to new financial challenges and opportunities that may arise in the future.

Now that we have covered topics like "the origins of money" and "importance of financial literacy," let's look at the role of banks and central banks.

ROLE OF BANKS AND CENTRAL BANKS

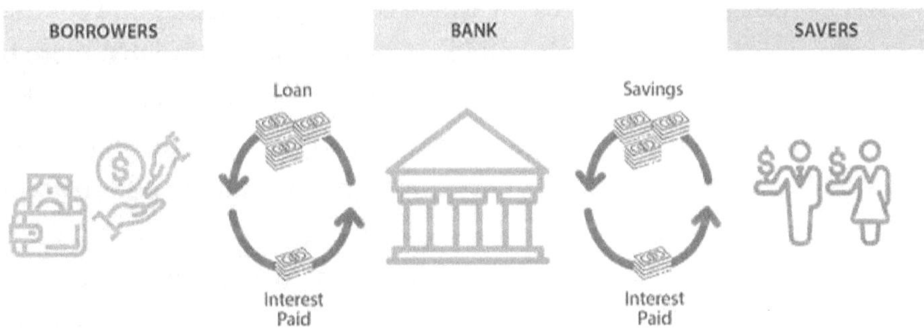

Banks serve as middlemen between depositors and borrowers, facilitating the flow of money throughout the economy. Banks receive deposits from depositors and use those funds to lend money to borrowers like people, companies, and governments. Banks are essential in fostering economic growth and development because they link those with extra cash to those who need financing. They promote entrepreneurship and job creation by enabling people to save and businesses to invest. Additionally, banks guarantee the integrity and security of deposited money, fostering trust in the financial system. Banks' role as intermediaries helps to ensure that capital is allocated efficiently, enabling the achievement of financial objectives as well as the overall stability and prosperity of the economy.

For instance, let's consider the example of personal loans in India. Personal loans typically have interest rates of around 17%, compared to depositor interest rates of 8–9% on average. The difference between these rates allows banks to earn a margin known as the **interest rate spread**. This margin represents the earnings that banks use for a variety of things, including paying employee salaries, maintaining infrastructure, and covering operational costs.

Central Banks – Almost every country has its own central bank. For example, India's central bank is the Reserve Bank of India, and the USA's central bank is The Federal Reserve. Now we will discuss the three main functions of the central bank.

1. Issuing Currency

Currency issuance is the process by which central banks create and control the money we use, such as coins and banknotes. They ensure that there is enough money for us to use in our daily transactions. Central banks also design money with special features that make it difficult to counterfeit. They withdraw old or damaged currency from circulation and replace it with new, fresh currency. Central banks do all of this to keep the economy running smoothly and to ensure that we can trust the money we use.

2. Monetary Policy

Central banks are in charge of creating and implementing monetary policy. They control the money supply using different methods such as interest rates, reserve requirements, and open market operations to accomplish specified goals such as price stability, low inflation, and sustainable economic growth.

3. Foreign Exchange Management

Central banks oversee a nation's foreign exchange reserves, intervening in currency markets to stabilise their domestic currency's value or rectify imbalances. This entails buying or selling foreign currency in order to influence exchange rates and promote economic stability.

EXPLORING DIVERSE MONETARY AND EXCHANGE RATE SYSTEMS

Gold Standard – The gold standard, a pivotal monetary system that shaped global economies during the 19th and early 20th centuries, was a currency framework in which a nation's money supply was directly linked to and backed by a specific quantity of gold reserves held by the government or central bank. This fundamental connection between currency and precious metal provided a foundation for stability and predictability in financial transactions and played a pivotal role in international trade.

Advantages:

1. Currency Stability – As the currencies were pegged to a certain amount of gold in the country's reserve, the value of the currency remained stable. This stability boosted confidence in the financial system and encouraged long-term financial planning.

2. International Trade – The gold standard promoted international trade as there was minimal fluctuation in currency markets (forex markets) since the currencies were artificially pegged to gold.

Disadvantages:

1. Limitations of Gold Supply – A notable disadvantage of the gold standard was its susceptibility to gold supply limitations. The system's

stability hinged on a consistent influx of gold, and any disruptions in gold production or availability could severely constrain a nation's ability to manage its currency effectively. In times of economic growth or crisis, the rigidity of the gold standard meant that the money supply could not be adjusted to accommodate changing financial needs, leading to potential economic hardships. This limitation underscored the vulnerability of the gold standard to external factors that were beyond the control of individual governments and central banks, ultimately contributing to its downfall.

2. Economic Constraints – Paradoxically, while the gold standard promoted stability, it sometimes imposed economic hardships during periods of growth. The limited money supply could hinder economic expansion by restricting the availability of credit and constraining investment opportunities. In times of economic prosperity, when demand for capital surged, the gold standard's fixed money supply often led to higher interest rates. This increased the cost of borrowing for businesses and individuals, reducing investments and leading to job loss. The rigidity of the gold standard's money supply became particularly evident during periods of industrial and economic expansion, underscoring the inherent tension between stability and adaptability in the monetary system.

Fiat Currency – Fiat currency is money that has value simply because a government declares it to be so. Unlike previous currencies, such as gold or silver-backed systems, fiat currency is not backed by a physical commodity. Its worth is determined by the trust and confidence of those who use it. Fiat currency is issued by governments and central banks and designated as legal tender, which means it must be accepted as a valid form of payment for debts and transactions within a given country. This means that there is no check on how much currency a central bank can issue. This may lead to inflation or deflation.

A. Inflation – Inflation is a fundamental concept in economics that touches the lives of individuals, businesses, and governments alike. It refers to the continuous increase in the general price level of goods and services in an economy over time. In simpler terms, it means that, on average, the things we buy tend to become more expensive as time goes on. While some level of inflation is considered normal and even beneficial for economic growth, understanding its causes, effects, and management is crucial for making informed financial decisions. Let's look into the causes of inflation.

Demand-Pull Inflation – One primary cause of inflation is excess demand for goods and services in an economy. When consumers and businesses collectively increase their spending, it can outstrip the economy's capacity to produce those goods and services. This leads to a demand-supply imbalance, causing prices to rise. It's essentially too much money chasing too few goods, often associated with economic growth and a booming business cycle.

Cost-Push Inflation – Another significant factor is cost-push inflation. This occurs when the costs of production for businesses increase. For instance, rising raw material prices, higher wages, or increased energy costs can lead companies to raise their prices to maintain profitability. This type of inflation is often driven by external factors and can be challenging to control.

Wage-Price Spiral – Another factor that contributes to inflation is the wage-price spiral. It happens when there is a never-ending cycle of rising wages and prices. Workers demand higher wages in order to keep up with the rising cost of living. In turn, businesses raise prices to maintain profit margins, passing on higher labour costs to customers. This situation creates a self-perpetuating cycle in which wages and prices continue to push each other upward, contributing to the economy's inflationary pressures. Breaking this cycle can be difficult for policymakers because it frequently necessitates addressing both wage and price dynamics at the same time.

Monetary Policy – The policies implemented by central banks can have a significant impact on inflation. When a central bank increases the money supply rapidly, typically through actions like lowering interest rates or engaging in quantitative easing, it can fuel inflation. This is because there is more money available in the economy for consumers and businesses to spend, leading to increased demand for goods and services. When demand exceeds supply, prices tend to rise. Conversely, tightening monetary policy by raising interest rates is a common strategy to combat inflation by reducing spending and slowing economic growth.

Supply Shocks – Inflation can be triggered by supply shocks, which are unexpected events that disrupt the supply of goods and services. Natural disasters, geopolitical conflicts, or abrupt changes in energy prices can disrupt production and distribution chains. When supply is constrained, it can lead to scarcity, causing prices to surge. These supply-side shocks can be temporary or permanent, depending on the nature of the event, and can have a significant impact on inflation rates and people's lives.

Exchange Rates – Exchange rate movements can influence inflation, particularly in countries heavily reliant on imports. When a domestic currency loses value, it can result in imported goods becoming more expensive. This happens because you need more of the local currency to buy the same amount of foreign goods. This can directly add to inflationary pressures by driving up the prices of imported items. These higher prices can have a ripple effect throughout the entire economy, impacting the overall cost of living.

B. Deflation – Deflation is an economic phenomenon characterised by a sustained decrease in the general price level of goods and services within an economy. It stands in contrast to inflation, which is the opposite – a continuous increase in prices. While a moderate and controlled level of inflation is generally considered normal in most modern economies, deflation can be a cause for concern and is often seen as an undesirable economic condition.

Decreased Consumer Demand – One significant cause of deflation is a decline in consumer demand. When people become uncertain about their financial future or are cautious due to economic hardships, they tend to cut back on spending. This reduced appetite for goods and services causes businesses to lower their prices to attract customers, ultimately leading to deflationary pressures. In this scenario, it's a reflection of individuals' and households' anxieties about their own financial stability, which ripple through the broader economy.

Debt Deflation – High levels of debt can contribute to deflation. When borrowers struggle to repay their loans due to economic difficulties, they cut back on spending to prioritise debt repayment. This reduction in spending creates a deflationary cycle as businesses respond by lowering prices to entice consumers. The human dimension here involves the struggles and sacrifices individuals and businesses make to manage their debts during tough economic times.

Floating Exchange – A floating exchange rate, also referred to as a flexible exchange rate, operates on the principle of letting market forces, like supply and demand in the foreign exchange market, determine the value of a currency. In this setup, the government or central bank doesn't actively step in to uphold a specific exchange rate. Instead, the exchange rate freely moves up and down depending on the prevailing market dynamics.

Floating exchange rates come with a number of benefits. They naturally adapt to shifts in economic fundamentals, thus aiding in the maintenance of trade balance and overall economic stability. Moreover, they provide policymakers with greater room to manoeuvre, enabling them to pursue autonomous monetary policies to tackle domestic economic issues. However, it's worth noting that floating exchange rates can be more prone to fluctuations and unpredictability, potentially causing uncertainty for businesses engaged in international trade.

Now, let's explore some real-life examples to better grasp the ideas mentioned earlier.

CASE STUDY 1:

CRISIS AND CURRENCY CHAOS – THE WEIMAR HYPERINFLATION SAGA

The economic crisis of hyperinflation in the Weimar Republic was a devastating event marked by a complex interplay of factors. After World War I, Germany grappled with the hefty burden of war reparations imposed by the Treaty of Versailles, amounting to 132 billion gold marks—an amount that far exceeded the nation's economic capacity in the aftermath of the war. The Weimar Republic, leading the German government, faced the formidable challenge of meeting these reparations amidst the struggle of the country's industrial and agricultural sectors to recover from the war's impact.

Initially, efforts were made to finance reparations through conventional means like taxation and loans. However, the post-war disillusionment, political instability, and resistance to increased taxation hindered these attempts. In a desperate move to bridge the fiscal gap, the government resorted to the printing press, resulting in an uncontrolled expansion of the money supply.

This imprudent monetary policy, coupled with a lack of corresponding growth in productive capacity, set the stage for hyperinflation. As the government flooded the economy with an ever-increasing quantity of banknotes, the value of the German mark plummeted at an alarming rate. The hyperinflationary spiral began around 1921, with prices doubling every few months. However, the situation rapidly worsened, reaching a peak in 1923 when prices were doubling not monthly, but every few days. This drastic escalation rendered the German mark nearly worthless, with citizens resorting to using wheelbarrows full of cash for routine transactions.

200 billion German Marks

The social consequences of hyperinflation were profound. The German middle class, historically a stabilising force, bore the brunt of the crisis. Savings were obliterated, pensions rendered worthless, and fixed incomes became insufficient to cover basic necessities. The erosion of wealth and financial security led to widespread social unrest, with citizens facing not only economic hardship but also a loss of faith in the stability of their society.

Efforts to mitigate the crisis emerged with the appointment of Gustav Stresemann as Chancellor in 1923. Under Stresemann's leadership and with Hjalmar Schacht as the currency commissioner, the introduction of the Rentenmark backed by tangible assets, along with subsequent economic reforms, provided a temporary reprieve. The establishment of the Reichsbank and the implementation of the Dawes Plan in 1924 aimed to further stabilise the German economy.

While these measures technically marked the end of hyperinflation, the scars of the crisis persisted. The traumatic experience fostered a deep-seated distrust of paper currency and a preference for tangible assets like real estate and gold. Moreover, the political consequences lingered, contributing to the fragility of the Weimar Republic and paving the way for the rise of the Nazi regime.

In essence, the hyperinflation crisis of the Weimar Republic was a convergence of economic mismanagement, exacerbated by the burdens of war reparations and socio-political turmoil. The unbridled printing of money, while temporarily easing financial pressures, precipitated an economic catastrophe with far-reaching consequences for German society and politics. This in-depth examination underscores the intricate web of factors that coalesced to create one of the most infamous hyperinflation episodes in history. Hyperinflation destroyed the political and economic landscape of the Weimar Republic.

CASE STUDY 2

ZIMBABWE'S ECONOMIC TURMOIL – UNRAVELLING THE IMPACT OF HYPERINFLATION

In the late 2000s, Zimbabwe faced a severe hyperinflation crisis, mainly due to serious mishandling of money by the government. Robert Mugabe's administration printed an excessive amount of money to cover budget deficits, especially for costly military actions and the controversial land reform programme. This flood of Zimbabwean dollars into the economy, without a corresponding increase in goods and services, triggered an unprecedented hyperinflationary spiral.

The government's financial recklessness was evident in the issuance of banknotes with ever-increasing denominations, reaching astronomical figures in the millions, billions, and even trillions. The sheer volume of money in circulation, coupled with its rapidly decreasing value, eroded public trust in the Zimbabwean dollar. As people saw their savings disappear and the purchasing power of their wages drop overnight, there was a surge in demand for foreign currencies and alternative forms of exchange.

The collapse of the agricultural sector, linked to Mugabe's land reforms, played a crucial role in the monetary crisis. Seizing white-owned commercial farms without compensation led to a sharp decline in agricultural productivity. This once-thriving sector, a cornerstone of Zimbabwe's economy, crumbled, causing food shortages and a loss of export revenue. The inability to produce and export goods further strained the country's foreign exchange reserves, worsening the economic downturn.

To address the hyperinflation crisis, the Reserve Bank of Zimbabwe resorted to printing higher denominations of currency, rendering the Zimbabwean dollar practically worthless. However, these actions lacked a foundation in sound monetary principles, failing to address the root causes of hyperinflation, such as the need for fiscal discipline and structural economic reforms. The combination of excessive money supply and a shrinking economy created a self-perpetuating cycle of hyperinflation.

As hyperinflation increased, the monetary system itself became a source of instability. The rapid depreciation of the Zimbabwean dollar led to frequent price adjustments, causing logistical challenges for businesses and complicating financial transactions. The chaos extended beyond physical banknotes, affecting electronic transactions and digital representations of the currency.

Ultimately, in 2009, the Zimbabwean government abandoned its own currency, adopting a multi-currency system with foreign currencies like the US dollar and South African rand. While this brought some stability, it highlighted the profound failure of monetary and fiscal policies that caused the crisis. The scars of hyperinflation continued to impact monetary policy in the following years, emphasising the crucial need for responsible financial management to maintain the integrity of a nation's currency. The Zimbabwean hyperinflation saga serves as a stark lesson on the consequences of uncontrolled monetary expansion and the importance of prudent economic governance.

CASE STUDY 3:

DEFLATION'S IMPACT ON DAILY LIVES: A STORY OF JAPAN'S ECONOMIC STRUGGLE

Japan went through a tough economic period known as the "Lost Decade," lasting from the 1990s well into the 2000s. It all began with the bursting of Japan's asset price bubble in the late 1980s, marked by skyrocketing real estate and stock prices. This speculative frenzy became unsustainable, and when the bubble burst in the early 1990s, it had a profound impact on the Japanese economy.

The aftermath revealed the financial vulnerability of the Japanese system. Banks, heavily invested in inflated assets, found themselves dealing with a load of non-performing loans as asset values plummeted. This triggered a significant banking crisis, disrupting normal credit market functions. The aftermath led to a credit crunch, as banks, grappling with the fallout of bad loans, became cautious about extending credit. This, in turn, stifled business expansion and investment, worsening the economic downturn.

Japan's response to the crisis involved a mix of fiscal and monetary measures. Initially, there was some denial about the severity of the economic challenges, and policy responses tended to be reactive rather than proactive. Pouring substantial public funds into the banking sector aimed to prevent a complete financial collapse, but these efforts fell short of fostering a robust recovery. The nuanced interplay between fiscal and monetary policies during this period highlights the complexities of addressing a multifaceted economic crisis.

Deflation became a prominent and enduring feature of Japan's economic landscape during this time. Falling asset prices, coupled with weakened consumer demand, led to a prolonged period of declining prices. In a deflationary environment, consumers expected lower prices in the future, causing them to delay purchases, further depressing economic activity and creating a self-reinforcing cycle of contraction. Conventional policy tools struggled to break this deflationary spiral, illustrating the challenges of managing an economy gripped by entrenched deflationary expectations.

Structural issues added another layer of complexity to Japan's economic challenges. Demographic shifts, including an ageing population and a declining workforce, posed significant challenges to sustained economic growth. These demographic trends resulted in reduced productivity and limited potential for economic expansion. Additionally, the rigid labour market and slow pace of structural reforms hindered the economy's adaptability and innovation, impeding the prospects for a robust recovery.

Monetary policy played a crucial role in Japan's efforts to combat deflation. The Bank of Japan implemented unconventional measures, such as zero interest rate policies and quantitative easing, to stimulate economic activity and raise inflation. However, these measures faced limitations, and the central bank grappled with the persistent challenge of achieving its inflation target.

The term "Lost Decade" is somewhat misleading, as the economic challenges persisted beyond a mere ten years. While Japan did eventually emerge from the worst of the economic downturn, the recovery was slow and fragile. The prolonged economic struggles prompted a reassessment of policy approaches and a deeper examination of the structural factors influencing Japan's economic trajectory.

The legacy of Japan's deflationary era extends beyond its borders, shaping global economic thought and policy discussions. Policymakers worldwide have learned from Japan's experience in addressing economic crises, dealing with deflation, and implementing structural reforms. Japan's case serves as a rich and complex case study, contributing to a nuanced understanding of the intricate interplay between monetary, fiscal, and structural policies in navigating prolonged periods of economic stagnation.

BANKING

BANKING SERVICES

First, let's talk in brief about the different types of accounts.

Savings Account

Savings accounts represent financial instruments proffered by banks and other financial institutions, facilitating individuals in securely depositing and safeguarding their funds while garnering a modest interest on their balances. Upon the initiation of a savings account, an individual essentially forges a relationship with the bank, entrusting the deposition of funds into the account, with the bank reciprocating by remitting interest on the balance over time. Though the interest rate – compounded annually – is typically more conservative compared to alternative investment avenues, savings accounts are acknowledged for their low-risk profile. Account holders retain the flexibility to access their funds at their discretion through withdrawals or transfers, rendering savings accounts a liquid and adaptable means of financial preservation.

The interest accrual is conventionally computed on either a monthly or annual basis, and it is imperative to recognise that the interest earned is subject to taxation. While savings accounts may not yield substantial returns in comparison to more venturesome investments, they function as a dependable and secure method for individuals to allocate funds, establish an emergency fund, or pursue short-term financial objectives.

Current Account

Current accounts, alternatively referred to as checking accounts in certain regions, constitute financial instruments extended by banks and other financial institutions to both individuals and businesses. These accounts are strategically designed to streamline routine financial transactions, encompassing activities such as deposits, withdrawals, and transfers. Unlike savings accounts, current accounts typically do not yield substantial interest on deposited funds. Instead, their primary function is to furnish a convenient and easily accessible platform for day-to-day financial engagements.

Accountholders are provided with a chequebook, a debit card, and access to online banking services. These tools empower individuals and businesses to deposit funds into the account, issue cheques for payments, withdraw cash from ATMs, and execute electronic transactions. Current accounts commonly impose little to no restrictions on the frequency of transactions, rendering them well-suited for recurrent financial activities.

Moreover, current accounts may incorporate overdraft facilities, affording accountholders the ability to expend beyond the actual account balance, subject to a predetermined limit. However, it is noteworthy that overdrafts typically incur fees and interest charges. Current accounts hold paramount significance in the management of day-to-day expenditures, bill payments, and routine financial transactions. They provide a heightened level of liquidity, ensuring prompt access to funds as necessitated. In sum, current accounts play a foundational role in facilitating the smooth flow of financial operations for both individuals and businesses.

Fixed/Term Deposits

Fixed deposits, commonly known as term deposits, represent financial instruments extended by banks and other financial institutions, providing individuals with the opportunity to invest a lump sum amount for a predetermined duration at a fixed interest rate. Embraced for their low-risk nature, fixed deposits appeal to conservative investors seeking a steady and foreseeable return on their savings.

Upon the establishment of a fixed deposit account, an individual commits to leaving a specific sum of money with the bank for a stipulated tenure, ranging from a few months to several years. The interest rate is established at the time of deposit and remains unaltered throughout the agreed-upon period. In contrast to savings accounts where interest rates may fluctuate, fixed deposits proffer a guaranteed and often elevated interest rate.

A distinctive feature of fixed deposits lies in the immobility of funds for the duration of the term. Premature withdrawals prior to the maturity date may incur penalties or a reduction in the accrued interest. This characteristic renders fixed deposits suitable for individuals with specific financial objectives who can allocate funds without requiring immediate access to them.

Upon the term's conclusion, the principal amount, along with the amassed interest, is reimbursed to the investor. The interest may be disbursed periodically (e.g., monthly, quarterly) or compounded and remitted at the term's conclusion. Fixed deposits furnish a secure avenue for capital growth while ensuring a known and predictable return, rendering them an appealing choice for risk-averse investors in pursuit of stability and capital preservation.

Now that we have it out of our way, let's delve into the world of international banking and finance. Let's first start with the World Bank and the IMF (International Monetary Fund).

BRETTON WOODS AND THE WORLD BANK

The Bretton Woods Institution comprises two significant international entities—the International Monetary Fund (IMF) and the World Bank—originating from the United Nations Monetary and Financial Conference held in Bretton Woods, New Hampshire, USA, in July 1944. This pivotal conference sought to formulate a new global monetary and financial framework in the aftermath of World War II, aiming to foster economic stability, prevent a recurrence of a worldwide economic downturn, and facilitate post-war reconstruction.

Post-World War II, the global economy encountered substantial challenges, prompting representatives from 44 allied nations to convene at the Bretton Woods conference to address these issues. The outcome was the establishment of the International Monetary Fund (IMF) and the International Bank for Reconstruction and Development (IBRD), later integrated into the World Bank Group. These institutions were formally instituted in 1945 with the overarching objective of promoting international economic collaboration and development.

The IMF was crafted to uphold exchange rate stability, encourage the growth of international trade, and extend short-term financial aid to member nations grappling with balance of payments challenges. Conversely, the World Bank aimed to provide extended loans in support of the reconstruction and development of war-torn nations, primarily in Europe. Over the years, both institutions expanded their mandates to tackle evolving global economic complexities.

The breakdown of the Bretton Woods system can be traced back to a sequence of economic challenges and policy adjustments, notably spearheaded by the United States under the leadership of President Richard Nixon. In 1971, confronted with economic difficulties such as heightened inflation and a burgeoning trade deficit, President Nixon took a pivotal step by declaring the suspension of the convertibility of the U.S. dollar into gold. This landmark decision, known as the Nixon Shock, signified the conclusion of the fixed exchange rate system established under Bretton Woods.

Within the Bretton Woods framework, the U.S. dollar was linked to gold, and other major currencies were tethered to the U.S. dollar. Nevertheless, escalating economic pressures prompted the United States to relinquish the gold standard in favour of a system featuring flexible exchange rates. This shift allowed currencies to fluctuate based on market forces, eliminating fixed exchange rates.

The abandonment of the gold standard carried profound implications for the international monetary system. The transition to flexible exchange rates ushered in a new era of currency fluctuations and increased volatility in financial markets. While affording countries greater flexibility in managing their monetary policies, this move brought forth multiple challenges, including uncertainties in exchange rates and escalated risks for global trade.

In the aftermath of the Nixon Shock, the International Monetary Fund (IMF) recalibrated its role to align with the altered economic landscape. Shifting its focus from promoting exchange rate stability, the IMF redirected its efforts towards assisting member countries in navigating the complexities introduced by flexible exchange rates. This adjustment marked a significant departure from the original vision of Bretton Woods but underscored the imperative of adapting to the ever-evolving global economic milieu.

Loans play a significant role in the World Bank's financial toolkit, primarily administered through the International Bank for Reconstruction and Development (IBRD). The IBRD extends loans to middle-income and creditworthy low-income countries, offering financial support for a broad spectrum of development projects and initiatives. Here are key facets illuminating the operational dynamics of World Bank loans:

5. Concessional Financing: While IBRD loans don't adhere strictly to the concessional model, they often incorporate features like low-interest rates, extended repayment periods, and grace periods. These terms render the loans more advantageous for borrowing countries, enabling them to access funds at comparatively lower costs than those available in commercial markets.

6. Project-Focused Financing: World Bank loans are earmarked for specific projects, allocated to finance initiatives identified by the borrowing country. These projects span diverse sectors such as infrastructure (e.g., roads, bridges, and energy), education, healthcare, and social welfare. The objective is to tackle specific development challenges and contribute to sustainable economic growth.

7. Economic and Policy Reforms: In certain instances, World Bank loans are linked to economic and policy reforms within the borrowing country. These loans may be contingent on the implementation of structural adjustments, governance enhancements, or other measures aimed at improving the overall economic landscape and fostering long-term development.

8. Flexible Repayment Terms: The IBRD collaborates closely with borrowing countries to customise repayment terms based on their specific circumstances. This flexibility assists countries in managing their debt obligations without imposing undue strain on their economies. Repayment schedules often span several decades, facilitating gradual repayment and alleviating immediate financial burdens.

9. Leveraging Additional Resources: World Bank loans frequently serve as a catalyst for additional resources, both from the private sector and other development partners. This leveraging effect proves crucial for addressing large-scale projects or initiatives where the financial requirements surpass what the World Bank can independently provide.

10. Graduation to Commercial Markets: As countries advance in their economic development, the aim is for them to transition from relying on concessional financing from institutions like the World Bank to accessing capital from commercial markets. This shift reflects the success of development efforts and the heightened creditworthiness of the borrowing country.

11. Risk Mitigation: Through its loans, the World Bank often plays a pivotal role in mitigating risks associated with development

projects. By offering financial support and technical expertise, the bank helps diminish perceived risks for private sector investors, encouraging their involvement in projects that might otherwise be considered too uncertain.

12. World Bank loans, characterised by favourable terms and a project-focused approach, strive to contribute to the long-term development and poverty reduction goals of borrowing countries. The emphasis on flexibility, sustainability, and leveraging additional resources underscores the World Bank's commitment to addressing the diverse and evolving needs of its member countries.

IMF

Aspect	World Bank	IMF
Purpose and focus	Reduce poverty and support sustainable development in developing countries.	Ensure Global monetary stability and facilitate economic cooperation.
Main Activity	Financing long term development projects, such as infrastructure, education, and healthcare.	Surveillance of global economic trends, providing short term financial assistance to countries facing balance of payments problems.
Financial Assistance	Provides loans and grants for development projects	Provides short-term financial assistance to member countries facing balance of payments problems, often with conditions attached.

Borrower Focus	Focuses on developing countries.	Provides assistance to all member countries facing economic challenges, including both developed and developing nations
Time Horizon	Emphasises long-term development.	Addresses short-to-medium-term economic challenges and crises.
Conditions for Assistance	Often includes conditions related to project implementation and policy reforms to ensure sustainability and effectiveness.	Typically includes economic policy conditions and structural reforms to address the root causes of economic imbalances.
Governance Structure	Consists of the International Bank for Reconstruction and Development (IBRD) and the International Development Association (IDA).	Governed by its member countries, with voting power determined by financial contributions (quotas).

INVESTMENT & SPECULATION

Benjamin Graham, the father of value investing, defines an investment as: "An investment operation is one which, upon thorough analysis, promises safety of principal and an adequate return. Operations not meeting these are speculative."

This means that we should thoroughly analyse a company, and the soundness of the underlying company and its management. We must hedge our bets and try to ensure we minimise losses. We must not fall into the trap of expecting extraordinary results. Expecting adequate results is the key.

Every member of the public who has a small sum invested in the market does not become an investor. There has to be proper research and reasoning behind buying a security (stock). Buying and selling securities based on emotional conviction or hoping that a stock of XYZ will make you rich overnight is not investing. It is speculation. Speculating while thinking that you're investing is the gravest mistake any person investing can ever make. Whenever there is a sudden market downturn, newspapers/media outlets use euphemisms like "Reckless Investors". Everyone who purchases or sells a stock is not an investor.

When a person is buying a new refrigerator, TV, car etc., he/she does at least some kind of research. They look up 5-6 different brands, compare their potential savings etc. But when it comes to buying/selling a security, they rely on their instincts.

One potential solution that is commonly suggested by many financial professionals is to keep two brokerage accounts: one for investing based on solid research and reasoning, and the other for speculative purposes.

Speculation is almost like gambling. Just like gambling, speculation is a lot of fun given that you're ahead in the game. As the common saying goes, the house always wins; in the case of trading/speculation, the exchange and broker always win, as they are the ones who make money regardless of whether or not you make money. Therefore, in this case, it is advisable to start a second brokerage account, in which you will make a deposit of a certain amount of money depending on your situation, and you will trade/speculate from it. Remember to never add extra money to this account and to never trade on your main investment account.

PASSIVE/DEFENSIVE INVESTORS

In the past (50s- 70s), it was recommended that a person should divide his holdings between bonds and stocks. It was also recommended that one should not keep more than 75% of his holdings in either stocks or bonds. The simplest choice was to have a 50-50 split between the two. If a person felt that the market was dangerously high, he would choose to increase his bond holdings while reducing his securities holdings. Conversely, if he felt that the market was too low and was a prime time to invest, he would choose to increase his stock holdings while systematically reducing his bond holdings.

In those days, treasury bills/bonds could give the investor almost 3-4 percent. And the dividend yield from common/blue-chip stocks used to be around 2.5-4 percent. So, a combination of both these could give the investor a safe 6-8 percent return. It should be noted that inflation in those times was only around 1.5 percent. That indirectly implies that a return of 7% is considered to be good. The delta (difference) between the return and inflation was

$$\Delta \%return = 7 - 1.5 \approx 5.5\%$$

Nowadays (2023), a 10-year treasury bill yields 3.9 percent, and the overall market increases by about 10 percent. It should also be noted that the inflation rate in 2022 was around 8% (2023 data not available yet).

Therefore, a combination of both would yield around 13% YoY (year on year). That makes the delta

Δ %return = 13 - 8 $\approx$ 5%. A decrease in inflation rates would make investing much more attractive.

A defensive investor may use dollar-cost averaging, which means that he invests in a good blue-chip stock or an index fund periodically with the same number of dollars. In this way, he buys more shares when the market is comparatively low and vice versa.

In this manner, a passive/defensive investor can expect his overall holdings to grow by 5% YoY, without taking any major risk or making any hard decisions.

AGGRESSIVE/ACTIVE INVESTOR

The aggressive investor, who manages his portfolio actively, will obviously want greater returns than the passive investor. This is all well and fine. One thing he must ensure is that he does not perform worse than his counterpart.

Before we delve further, there are a few ways in which a person can expect higher returns:

1. Trading: This means the same as speculation, short-term buying and selling of securities. Anyone who trades must try to ensure that they don't lose all their money, and they don't get addicted to it.
2. Purchasing shares in companies that they think are set to perform better within a given time frame, for example during COVID-19, the healthcare stocks zoomed.
3. Buying stocks in companies that are going to publish quarterly earnings reports, assuming that the report is better than the previous quarter.

4. Buying up-and-coming sectors, in the early 70s it was computers and technology, nowadays is more inclined towards companies related to robotics, AI (artificial intelligence), etc.

5. Market timing is an active investment strategy centred on predicting the future direction of financial markets and making investment decisions accordingly. This strategy rests on the belief that it's possible to identify optimal entry and exit points to capitalise on anticipated market trends. Asset allocation decisions in market timing are based on short-term predictions of market movements, economic indicators, and other relevant factors. Investors using market timing may adjust their portfolio composition, moving into or out of specific asset classes like stocks, bonds, or cash, with the aim of maximising returns and minimising risk. Advocates of market timing argue that accurately forecasting market trends can enhance overall investment performance and shield portfolios from downturns. However, critics highlight the challenges and risks associated with market timing, emphasising the difficulty of consistently predicting market movements accurately. The unpredictability of global events, economic factors, and market sentiment makes it challenging for even seasoned investors to time the market consistently. Moreover, frequent trading involved in market timing can lead to higher transaction costs, tax implications, and potential underperformance due to missed opportunities or mistimed entries and exits.

6. Contrarian investing is a unique way to dive into the investment world. Instead of just going with the flow of what everyone else is doing, contrarian investors like to swim against the current market mood. They believe that the crowd isn't always on the money, and that's where the fun begins. The whole idea is to scout for chances in assets or markets that are, well, a bit out of fashion or going through a rough patch. It's like saying, "Hey, just because everyone's not into it right now doesn't mean it's not a good deal." It's all about looking at the market with a fresh pair of

eyes. Contrarians basically bet on the fact that when the market gets all gloomy and things are undervalued, it's like a secret stash of golden opportunities waiting to be discovered. They think that when people freak out about bad news, they might overreact, and that can mess with the prices. So, smart contrarians see this as a chance to jump in before things bounce back up.

It's not the easiest route, though. Going against the crowd can mess with your head, and you might need some serious patience. But successful contrarians know how to ride the waves, spot opportunities when others are seeing red flags, and play the waiting game until the market catches on to the hidden value they spotted from the start. It's like being the cool, calm surfer in the investment world, patiently waiting for the right wave to ride.

7. Momentum investing is like catching a wave in the stock market, relying on the belief that assets with recent strong performances will likely continue their winning streak. It's a forward-looking strategy that rides the momentum of price trends, assuming that securities moving up or down will keep heading in the same direction for a while. Using technical analysis, investors examine charts and indicators to spot assets showing signs of strength or weakness. The underlying principle is grounded in the idea that the market tends to react slowly to new information, providing opportunities for investors to profit from ongoing trends. While this approach can be applied to various asset classes, it contrasts with traditional value investing by focusing less on fundamentals and more on recent price movements. Despite its potential, momentum investing carries risks, as sudden market reversals and increased volatility are par for the course.

8. Hedging represents a sophisticated risk management strategy embraced by investors and businesses to safeguard against potential losses arising from unfavourable market movements. Essentially, it involves the strategic deployment of financial instruments or positions to counterbalance the impact of adverse price fluctuations

in an asset or portfolio. This strategic manoeuvre gains particular importance in volatile markets or uncertain economic landscapes where unforeseen events can expose entities to substantial financial risks. Investors typically employ derivatives like options or futures contracts to create hedges, establishing positions that move in the opposite direction to the assets they aim to protect. For example, an equity investor wary of potential market downturns might opt for put options to institute a mechanism for downside protection. Similarly, businesses engaged in international trade might use currency hedges to shield themselves from unfavourable exchange rate shifts. While hedging proves effective in risk management, it introduces its own intricacies. Investors need to carefully evaluate the costs of implementing hedges and consider potential trade-offs between protection and potential returns. Mastering the art of hedging requires a nuanced understanding of the specific risks at play (which we will discuss later) and the selection of appropriate instruments to achieve the desired risk reduction.

An example of hedging in the realm of stocks, without delving into futures or options, is exemplified by a pair trade. In a pair trade, an investor concurrently takes a long position (buying) in one stock and a short position (selling) in another stock within the same industry or sector. The aim is to leverage the relative performance between the two stocks while cushioning exposure to overarching market fluctuations.

Let's say an investor foresees that Stock A, a prominent technology company, will outshine Stock B, another technology company, in the short run. To guard against potential market turbulence or risks specific to the tech sector, the investor simultaneously assumes a long position in Stock A, expecting it to rise, and a short position in Stock B, anticipating its underperformance compared to Stock A.

In this scenario, if the technology sector undergoes a downturn due to broader market factors, the investor may still come out ahead if Stock A outperforms Stock B, thereby offsetting potential losses. The pair trade strategy enables the investor to focus on the relative strength or weakness between two closely linked stocks, offering a form of hedging against broader market movements within a specific sector.

There can always be human error in estimating the future earnings of any company. It may be due to personal biases. After all, as humans, we cannot predict the future.

TO BE NOTED

Simply because an investment technique or formula has proven successful within a specific timeframe doesn't guarantee its future performance, and its past success doesn't necessarily validate the correctness of the practitioner. Practices like day trading, chasing after trending stocks, and relying on internet financial gurus aren't considered genuine forms of investing. Trusting these so-called gurus doesn't equate to sound investment strategies. Following untested and risky trading systems is yet another pitfall. Just because a system worked by chance once or twice doesn't make it inherently correct or safe. The creators of such systems often attribute failures to "unexpected market events," but this doesn't absolve the lack of a proven and reliable foundation. It's crucial for investors to exercise caution, critically evaluate strategies, and be wary of approaches that lack a solid track record or are based on mere chance.

TIME COMMITMENT

Imagine managing your investments is like navigating a ship through ever-changing waters. For folks who are really hands-on, like active investors, it's a bit like steering that ship. They keep a close eye on everything happening in the markets, from economic trends to company news. It's not a set-it-and-forget-it deal; they're always tweaking things, adjusting where they've invested, and making decisions based on what's happening right now. It's a real-time commitment that takes time and effort.

Now, on the other side of things, you've got passive investors. They're more like kicking back on a sunny day, letting the ship cruise along. Once they've set their initial plan, they don't mess with it too much. Their portfolio just follows the overall performance of a chosen market index. It's all about the long game and not getting caught up in the day-to-day ups and downs. Passive investors check in every now and then to make sure their investments still match up with their chosen index and might make a few tweaks here and there. It's a more chill approach, steering clear of the constant adjustments and quick decisions that active management involves.

TRANSACTION COSTS

Let's put it in simpler terms. Think of transaction costs as the tolls you pay on your investment journey, and they're a big deal, especially when deciding between active and passive strategies. If you're the active type, buying and selling securities often, you've got to watch out for things like brokerage fees and bid-ask spreads – these are your toll booths, and they can really add up. If you're into quick trades or changing your investments a lot, these tolls can eat into your profits.

Now, picture passive investors as the easy riders. They stick to a buy-and-hold strategy, not messing with their investments too much. Since they're not hitting the toll booth as often, their costs are generally lower compared to the active crowd. Passive investing isn't just about cruising with the market; it's also about saving money in the long run. Lower tolls mean a more efficient and budget-friendly way to invest. This is a big deal, especially for those who want to protect their money and make the most out of their returns by avoiding unnecessary tolls from frequent trading. So, when it comes down to it, transaction costs are like the GPS that guides investors, shaping the path they take and highlighting the financial impact of their choices between active and passive strategies.

ECONOMICS

The University of Buffalo defines economics as "Economics is the study of scarcity and its implications for the use of resources, production of goods and services, growth of production and welfare over time, and a great variety of other complex issues of vital concern to society."

ECONOMICS AND DECISION MAKING & WHY WE SHOULD LEARN ECONOMICS

Economics plays a huge role in how we make decisions – whether we're individuals, businesses, or governments. It's like our trusty guide through the maze of choices and divvying up resources. At its core, economics helps us see, analyse, and make the most of what we've got when faced with our never-ending desires. Key ideas in economics, like scarcity, remind us that we've always got more wants than resources. So, we've got to think carefully about trade-offs and what really matters. Opportunity cost, another big concept, shows us the hidden costs of choosing one thing over another, nudging us to make decisions that bring the most happiness overall. And then there's marginal analysis, which helps us weigh the extra benefits and costs of our choices – a real game-changer in making smart decisions.

Zooming in, microeconomics looks at how individuals and businesses make choices. It dives into why we buy what we do, how companies decide what to produce, and the ins and outs of market dealings. Supply and demand, the rock stars of microeconomics, steer the ship when it comes to prices and amounts in markets, influencing how businesses set prices, decide what to produce, and use their resources.

Macroeconomics, on the other hand, zooms out to look at big-picture stuff like national income, employment, and inflation. Governments lean on these macro insights to shape policies that keep the economy steady, unemployment low, and growth sustainable.

In business, economic principles are the secret sauce behind market plans, pricing strategies, and investment decisions. The whole dance of supply chains, production schedules, and marketing moves follows the rhythm of economic principles. And for governments, knowing their economics is key to creating policies that balance things like controlling inflation, spurring economic growth, and taking care of society.

On a personal level, knowing a bit about economics helps us handle our money better – from budgeting to investing to planning for retirement. In a world that's always changing, understanding economics is like having a superpower that lets us see and understand the forces shaping our economic lives.

SCHOOLS OF ECONOMIC THOUGHT

Adam Smith, born in 1723 in Kirkcaldy, Scotland, is a towering figure in the intellectual landscape of the 18th century. Widely hailed as the "Father of Economics," his seminal work, "The Wealth of Nations," published in 1776, laid the groundwork for classical economics, influencing how we understand concepts like self-interest, competition, and the invisible hand guiding markets. However, Smith's intellectual legacy goes beyond economics; his earlier work, "The Theory of Moral Sentiments," delves into ethics and human nature, showcasing a nuanced thinker who bridged the realms of economic and moral philosophy. A true polymath, Smith's enduring influence resonates across disciplines, leaving an indelible mark on the minds of economists, philosophers, and policymakers.

SOME IMPORTANT CONCEPTS OUTLINED IN THE "WEALTH OF NATIONS."

Division of Labour

At its essence, the division of labour, as conceptualised by Adam Smith, revolves around breaking down the production process into specialised, repetitive tasks, assigning each worker a specific role in the overall chain. Using the iconic example of pin manufacturing, Smith contrasts the productivity of an individual attempting every step versus a team of specialised workers, each focused on a specific aspect. The outcome? A remarkable boost in productivity. Specialisation cultivates highly skilled workers, slashing the time and effort needed for each task. This not only amplifies overall output but also transforms work into a more mechanical and routine endeavour. According to Smith, this productivity surge isn't solely due to technology but is inherently tied to labour specialisation. It's not confined to manufacturing; it permeates all economic activities. Smith argues that broadening this principle across society results in wealth accumulation and prosperity. The transformative impact arises from the synergies of specialisation—each worker excelling in their role leads to a collective output surpassing individual self-sufficiency.

The division of labour thus becomes a driver for economic growth and prosperity, revealing the intricate link between specialisation, efficiency, and a nation's wealth. This is often attributed as inspiration behind Henry Ford's assembly line model.

The Invisible Hand

The concept of the "Invisible Hand" stands as a foundational principle in classical economic thought, serving as a metaphor for the unintended social benefits arising from individuals pursuing their self-interest in a competitive market. Adam Smith introduces this idea within the dynamics of markets, suggesting that individuals, in seeking personal gain, unknowingly contribute to the overall economic well-being of society, as if guided by an unseen force. The metaphor implies that, akin to an invisible hand orchestrating market action, the collective outcome benefits society.

At its core, the Invisible Hand concept posits that, in a free and competitive market, the pursuit of self-interest by individuals leads to positive outcomes for society. Activities like entrepreneurship, investment, and production, undertaken to maximise personal well-being, naturally result in the provision of goods and services that society demands. This process, governed by the forces of supply and demand, efficiently allocates resources. The Invisible Hand symbolises the self-regulating nature of markets, where the decentralised decisions of countless individuals collectively optimise resource allocation and maximise societal welfare.

The Invisible Hand operates through the price mechanism, where prices convey crucial information about scarcity and demand. High demand relative to availability raises prices, signalling profit opportunities to producers and prompting increased production. Conversely, surpluses lower prices, signalling producers to reallocate resources. This constant interplay, guided by individual self-interest, ensures resources flow to their most valued uses in society.

Crucially, the Invisible Hand requires competitive markets characterised by low barriers to entry and free exchange. Smith acknowledged that in the absence of competition or in distorted markets with monopolies, the optimal allocation of resources may be compromised.

While often associated with market dynamics, the Invisible Hand concept extends beyond economics. Smith's idea suggests that individuals, pursuing their interests in various life spheres, inadvertently contribute to the broader well-being of society. This insight underscores the benefits of individual freedom, innovation, and entrepreneurship in fostering societal progress.

Role of Competition

Adam Smith was all about competition in the market. He argued that in a competitive market, no single player gets to boss around and set prices. Prices are shaped by lots of buyers and sellers, each doing their thing to get the best deal for themselves. According to Smith, this competitive tug-of-war is great because it forces producers to up their game.

In a competitive market, companies have to improve their products, cut costs, and come up with cool new ideas to stay ahead. Plus, with lots of players in the game, no one gets a monopoly, keeping prices fair and making sure the market works for everyone. Smith believed that competition was like a superhero, keeping the market in check and sparking innovation.

Labour Theory of Value

Smith's thoughts on value were pretty interesting. He introduced this thing called the "labour theory of value." In a nutshell, he said the value of something is tied to the amount of work put into making it. This was a bit different from later ideas that said value depends on what people personally think about a product.

According to Smith, the value of a product wasn't just in how useful it was (value in use) but also in the work that went into making it (value in exchange). It's like saying, "Hey, this thing is worth a lot because a bunch of hard work went into making it." Even though later theories had different takes, Smith's labour theory of value left a mark on economic thinking.

Prices as Signals

Smith saw prices as powerful messages in the market. They're like arrows pointing to where resources are needed and where they're not. A rise in price signals high demand or low supply, telling producers, "Hey, make more of this!" Falling prices mean there's too much or not enough demand, signalling producers to adjust their game.

This role of prices as signals is a big deal because it helps people and businesses make smart choices about where to put their time, money, and effort. Smith thought of prices as messengers, constantly communicating important info about what's happening in the market.

Market Equilibrium

Picture a marketplace where the quantity demanded equals the quantity supplied, and things are in perfect balance. Adam Smith called this "market equilibrium." It's like the sweet spot where everyone's happy because what people want equals what's available, and prices are stable.

In a competitive market, Smith believed the invisible hand was always working behind the scenes to guide prices towards this equilibrium. It's a dynamic state where things adjust naturally over time. Changes in conditions prompt shifts in prices, and the market, according to Smith, has this cool ability to self-adjust and keep things in harmony.

Critique of Price Controls

Adam Smith wasn't a fan of anything messing with the natural flow of prices, especially government-imposed price controls. In "The Wealth of Nations," he argued that when you start setting price limits, you throw a wrench into the whole supply and demand dance. Price controls, whether putting a cap or a floor, mess with the signals that prices are supposed to send.

Smith's critique was rooted in the belief that markets, when left alone, can figure things out on their own. Interventions like price controls, he said, can have unintended consequences, messing with incentives for production and causing inefficiencies in how resources are used.

Wealth and Price Distortion

Smith had this grand idea about what true wealth is. It wasn't just about piling up shiny gold and silver; it was about creating value through efficient resource allocation and producing goods and services at competitive prices. According to Smith, policies that mess with prices, like putting up barriers to competition or restricting trade, mess with the process of creating wealth.

Price distortion, in Smith's eyes, disrupted the natural way markets generate wealth. By playing with prices, interventions could lead to misallocations of resources and slow down economic growth. Smith was all about letting markets do their thing and believed that competitive prices were key to the real creation of wealth.

Real vs. Nominal Prices

Smith had this cool idea about looking at prices in two ways: real and nominal. Real prices are like the actual buying power of your money, considering changes in the general price level. Nominal prices, on the other hand, are just the face values of goods and services.

This distinction was Smith's way of saying, "Hey, don't just look at the sticker price; consider what your money can actually buy." It set the stage for future discussions about inflation and how changes in the value of money impact the economy.

Prices and Market Dynamics

Throughout "The Wealth of Nations," Smith kept reminding everyone that markets are like living, breathing things. Prices aren't stuck; they change and respond to what's happening. Innovations, shifts in what people like, and new ways of making stuff – all these things influence prices.

Smith's big idea here was that markets are super flexible. They adapt to new info and changing conditions. This constant movement is what keeps markets efficient, ensuring that everyone – from producers to consumers – can adjust and thrive in a dynamic economic system.

Though we can't do justice to a 750-page book in mere 2-3 pages, we have covered the most important pointers in the book.

THEORY OF COMPARATIVE ADVANTAGE BY DAVID RICARDO

David Ricardo (1772–1823) was a British political economist and one of the most influential figures in classical economics. Born in London, Ricardo came from a wealthy Jewish family and began his career working in finance. However, he eventually turned his attention to economic theory and made significant contributions to the field.

The Genesis of Comparative Advantage

David Ricardo's Theory of Comparative Advantage isn't just a concept; it's a game-changer in the world of economic thinking. Born out of a critical examination of old-school mercantilist doctrines in the early 19th century, this theory challenges the idea that nations can only win at international trade if they hoard heaps of gold and precious metals. Ricardo, in his groundbreaking work "Principles of Political Economy and Taxation" (1817), introduces the concept of comparative advantage, shaking things up by suggesting that trade can be beneficial even if one country isn't the absolute champ in making everything.

Ricardo's move away from the old mercantilist beliefs is like a breath of fresh air in economic theory. He's saying, "Hey, let's consider how good we are at stuff compared to others." Comparative advantage, as Ricardo puts it, is all about looking at opportunity cost, telling economists and policymakers that the real perks of trade come from being more efficient, not just being better at everything.

Concepts and Opportunity Cost

At the heart of Ricardo's Theory of Comparative Advantage is this fancy thing called opportunity cost – a core economic principle that's all about weighing the alternatives you give up when you make a choice. In the world of international trade, it means looking at how efficiently you produce stuff. Ricardo's big idea is that nations should focus on making things where their opportunity cost is lower than their trade buddies. It's a smart approach that leads to using resources better and making everyone in the trade game happier.

Opportunity cost, thanks to Ricardo, changes how economists think about production efficiency and resource use. It's the key to understanding comparative advantage, reminding everyone that real trade gains happen when countries play to their strengths and specialise.

The Two-Country Model

Ricardo's illustrative example featuring England and Portugal serves as a didactic tool to unravel the complexities of comparative advantage. In this simplified two-country, two-commodity model,

Ricardo demonstrated how both nations could elevate their collective well-being through specialisation and trade. Portugal, possessing an absolute advantage in both wine and cloth production, showcased the paradox that even in such a scenario, mutual gains could be achieved.

The model underscores the win-win nature of international trade, dispelling the notion that one nation must be universally more efficient to derive benefits. By focusing on the goods with lower opportunity costs, nations can engage in complementary trade, wherein each specialises in what it does best, amplifying global productivity and consumption.

Real-World Applications

Ricardo's Theory of Comparative Advantage isn't just a bunch of ideas on paper; it's got street cred in the real world. While Ricardo's original model dealt with goods like wine and cloth, the principles stretch across the economic landscape, touching everything from services to tech to intellectual property. Countries are tuning into their unique strengths, getting into global value chains, and finding their groove through specialisation.

Look around, and you'll see Ricardo's theory at play in the contemporary scene. Developing nations are bringing their A-game with cost-effective labour or abundant natural resources, diving into global trade. Meanwhile, advanced economies are rocking the tech, innovation, and high-end services. Ricardo's theory is the compass guiding policymakers to craft trade policies that encourage openness and recognise that even less-developed nations can score big through specialisation and joining the global marketplace.

MAYNARD KEYNES

John Maynard Keynes, born in 1883 in Cambridge, England, is a notable figure in the field of economics, having significantly influenced economic perspectives during the tumultuous interwar period of the 20th century. Educated at Eton and Cambridge, Keynes traversed diverse professional realms, from civil service to journalism, before establishing himself as a transformative economic thinker.

His major work, "The General Theory of Employment, Interest, and Money," published in 1936, was a crucial milestone in economic thought. This work challenged classical economic paradigms and laid the groundwork for what would become known as Keynesian economics. The backdrop of the Great Depression, which defied conventional economic understanding, fuelled Keynes's revolutionary ideas.

Points following this are going to be more and more technical; it is not necessary to completely understand each and every point to be a successful investor, however, it's never bad to know.

Aggregate Demand & Supply

Aggregate Demand (AD) and Aggregate Supply (AS) are pivotal concepts in Keynesian economics, shedding light on the intricate dynamics that shape a nation's economic output, employment levels, and overall stability. Central to Keynesian theory is the idea that aggregate demand, encompassing consumption, investment, government spending, and net exports, plays a crucial role in determining economic performance. Keynes asserted that fluctuations in AD are the primary drivers of economic cycles, especially evident during periods of recession or depression.

On the flip side, Aggregate Supply (AS) reflects the total quantity of goods and services producers are willing and able to supply at different price levels. It is often categorised into short-run and long-run supply, with the former marked by inflexible prices and wages and the latter allowing for adjustments. The interaction between AD and AS establishes the equilibrium level of output and price levels in an economy.

In the Keynesian framework, the AD-AS model serves as a potent tool for comprehending economic dynamics. Essentially, Keynes argued that changes in AD, rather than price adjustments, are the primary catalysts for economic fluctuations. For example, during economic downturns, a decrease in consumer confidence or business investment can lead to an overall decline in demand, subsequently causing reduced production and a rise in unemployment. The AD-AS model illustrates this correlation, elucidating how a decrease in AD can result in diminished output and employment.

Keynes's emphasis on AD stems from the belief that prices and wages aren't always flexible, particularly in the short run. In contrast to the classical economic viewpoint that markets will naturally self-adjust, Keynes contended that intervention is essential during periods of economic distress. He advocated for active government policies, especially through fiscal measures, to manage AD and stabilise the economy. This approach is particularly relevant during recessions when households and businesses may curtail spending, leading to a decline in AD and subsequent economic contraction.

In the AD-AS model, Keynesian economics offers a unique perspective on the causes and remedies for economic downturns. Government intervention, such as increased spending or tax cuts, is viewed as a means to boost AD and stimulate economic activity. By directly influencing AD, Keynesian policies aim to restore full employment and economic stability. However, the effectiveness of such policies depends on the responsiveness of AD and the broader economic environment.

Moreover, the Keynesian viewpoint challenges the classical notion of a self-adjusting market. Rather than relying on price and wage flexibility to restore equilibrium, Keynesian economics underscores the potential for prolonged periods of unemployment and underutilisation of resources without appropriate government intervention. This emphasis on managing aggregate demand has profound implications for economic policy, particularly during times of crisis.

Keynesian Cross Model

The Keynesian Cross Model starts by distinguishing between two essential components: aggregate income and aggregate spending. This model assumes a closed economy, meaning there is no international trade, and simplifies economic agents to households and firms. Aggregate income represents the total earnings of households and firms, while aggregate spending includes consumption, investment, government expenditures, and net exports. The equilibrium in the model occurs when aggregate income equals aggregate spending.

A key element of the model is the consumption function, which outlines the relationship between disposable income and consumption. Keynes proposed that households don't spend their entire income but rather consume a fraction of it. This introduces the concept of autonomous consumption—spending that occurs even when income is zero—and the marginal propensity to consume (MPC)—the proportion of additional income that is spent. These concepts are crucial for understanding how changes in income impact spending patterns.

The Keynesian Cross Model also includes the concept of the expenditure function, representing total spending in the economy. It includes both autonomous spending, like government expenditures and investment, and induced spending, linked to changes in income. The model assumes that firms determine their production level based on the expected level of spending in the economy.

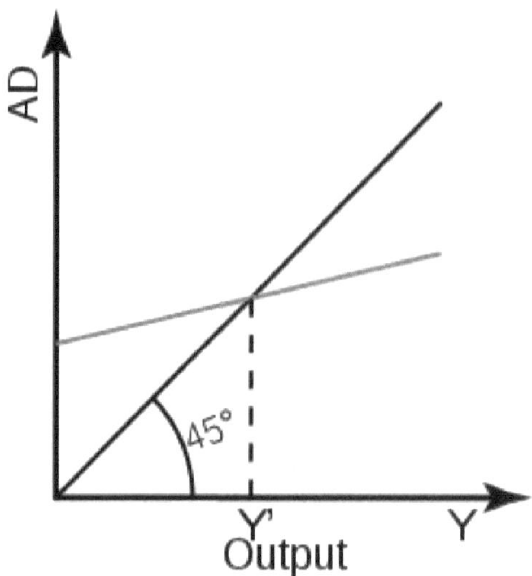

The interaction between the consumption function and the expenditure function forms the foundation of the Keynesian Cross Model. Graphically, the model is represented as a 45-degree line, known as the 45-degree line of equality, where the vertical axis represents aggregate spending, and the horizontal axis represents aggregate income. The slope of this line is equal to one, reflecting the equality between income and spending in equilibrium.

To delve deeper, consider a scenario where aggregate spending is below aggregate income. This disequilibrium incentivises firms to reduce production, leading to a decline in income. As income decreases, so does consumption, further widening the gap between income and spending. Conversely, if aggregate spending exceeds aggregate income, firms increase production to meet higher demand, leading to an expansion of income. This positive feedback loop illustrates the self-adjusting nature of the Keynesian Cross Model, where changes in spending have a multiplier effect on income, either contracting or expanding the economy.

The model introduces the concept of the expenditure multiplier, magnifying the impact of changes in spending on the overall economy. The multiplier effect arises from the interplay between changes in spending, changes in income, and changes in consumption. An initial injection of spending sets off a chain reaction, creating a cumulative effect on income larger than the initial spending.

The Keynesian Cross Model is not just theoretical; it's a practical tool for policymakers. It underscores the importance of managing aggregate demand for economic stability. During recessions, increasing government spending can stimulate economic activity by boosting aggregate demand. Conversely, during periods of inflation or excessive growth, reducing government spending can help kerb inflationary pressures.

Liquidity Preference and Interest Rates

Liquidity Preference delves into the demand for money and its different forms, shedding light on how individuals and firms decide between holding cash and interest-bearing assets. Keynes identified three motives behind the desire to hold money: the transactions motive, the precautionary motive, and the speculative motive.

The transactions motive refers to the need for money to facilitate day-to-day transactions. Individuals and businesses keep cash on hand as a medium of exchange for regular payment obligations, like purchasing goods and services. The precautionary motive involves holding money as a safeguard against unforeseen contingencies and uncertainties. Keynes argued that individuals maintain a certain amount of cash to cover unexpected expenses, creating a financial buffer against life's uncertainties. Lastly, the speculative motive introduces the element of interest rates. According to Keynes, investors hold money not only for transactions or precautionary reasons but also for speculative purposes, especially anticipating changes in the value of financial assets.

Keynes's Liquidity Preference theory asserts an inverse relationship between the demand for money and the interest rate. In simpler terms, as interest rates rise, the demand for money decreases, and vice versa. Understanding this relationship is fundamental to grasping the impact of monetary policy on the broader economy. Fluctuations in interest rates affect the level of investment and consumption, influencing overall economic output.

The speculative motive plays a crucial role in connecting liquidity preference to interest rates. Keynes suggested that individuals face a choice between holding money and interest-bearing assets, such as bonds. When interest rates are high, the opportunity cost of holding money increases, as individuals forgo potential interest earnings on alternative investments. Consequently, during periods of elevated interest rates, the speculative motive prompts a shift away from money holdings towards interest-bearing assets.

Conversely, when interest rates are low, the incentive to hold money becomes more appealing. The opportunity cost of forgoing interest income diminishes, and individuals may choose to hold more cash. This shift in preferences aligns with the inverse relationship between interest rates and the demand for money outlined in Liquidity Preference theory.

The implications of liquidity preference go beyond individual choices and resonate throughout the financial system, influencing monetary policy. Central banks, as custodians of monetary policy, recognise the interplay between interest rates and liquidity preference as a crucial determinant of economic conditions. In response to economic challenges, central banks may adjust interest rates to stimulate or restrain economic activity.

For instance, during economic downturns or recessions, central banks often lower interest rates to encourage borrowing, spending, and investment. This reduction in interest rates aligns with Keynes's liquidity preference theory, as it makes holding money relatively less attractive compared to investing in interest-bearing assets. This, in turn, stimulates economic activity by fostering increased consumption and investment.

Conversely, in times of inflationary pressures, central banks may raise interest rates to curb excessive spending and investment. The higher interest rates increase the opportunity cost of holding money, leading to a reduction in consumption and investment. Here, too, the central bank's actions reflect an understanding of liquidity preference dynamics and their role in shaping economic outcomes.

CLASSICAL VS KEYNESIAN

Aspect	Keynesian Economics	Classical Economics
Employment	Highlights the significance of involuntary unemployment and market imperfections. Keynesian economists posit that in the short run, wages and prices may exhibit rigidity, contributing to involuntary unemployment even in the absence of sufficient aggregate demand.	Endorses the self-adjusting characteristics of markets, viewing unemployment as a transient state. Classical economists contend that any unemployment is a result of factors like inflated wages, and they maintain that markets will naturally reach equilibrium in the long run.

Aggregate Supply & Deman	Focuses on managing aggregate demand to achieve full employment. Keynesians assert that managing demand is crucial, as the economy can remain below full employment due to inadequate demand.	Believes that aggregate supply adjusts to changes in demand, and markets will naturally reach equilibrium. Classical economists argue that markets will clear, and supply will adjust to meet demand over time.
Role of Government	Advocates for active government intervention, particularly through fiscal policy, to manage the economy and stabilise fluctuations.	Argues for limited government involvement, and expresses concerns that government intervention can lead to market distortions.

MILTON FRIEDMAN

Milton Friedman (1912-2006) stood as a distinguished American economist and Nobel laureate, earning widespread recognition as one of the most influential figures in 20th-century economics. Renowned for his unwavering support of free-market capitalism, Friedman's ideas wielded significant influence over economic policies and shaped political ideologies. His groundbreaking work, "A Monetary History of the United States," co-authored with Anna Schwartz, challenged established perspectives on the causes of the Great Depression. As a staunch proponent of limited government intervention, Friedman's commitment to individual freedom and free-market principles has left a lasting imprint on economic theory and public policy.

Quantity Theory of Money

The Quantity Theory of Money (QTM) stands as a fundamental concept in economics, aiming to unravel the connection between the money supply in an economy and the overall price level. Rooted in classical economic thought, the Quantity Theory of Money has evolved over the years, influencing economic policy and shaping our comprehension of inflation, monetary policy, and the broader macroeconomic landscape.

At its essence, the Quantity Theory of Money proposes a straightforward equation: $MV = PT$. Here, M represents the money supply, V is the velocity of money, P denotes the price level, and T signifies the volume of transactions in the economy. This equation encapsulates the notion that the total spending in an economy (MV) equals the total value of goods and services exchanged (PT). The theory posits that changes in the money supply directly impact the price level, assuming a constant velocity of money and a stable volume of transactions.

Historically, the Quantity Theory of Money found early champions in the works of classical economists like David Hume and John Locke. However, it was the monetarist school of thought, notably led by Irving Fisher and later popularised by Milton Friedman in the 20th century, that thrust the theory into the spotlight. Friedman, in particular, underscored the central bank's role in controlling the money supply to maintain price stability and prevent inflationary or deflationary pressures.

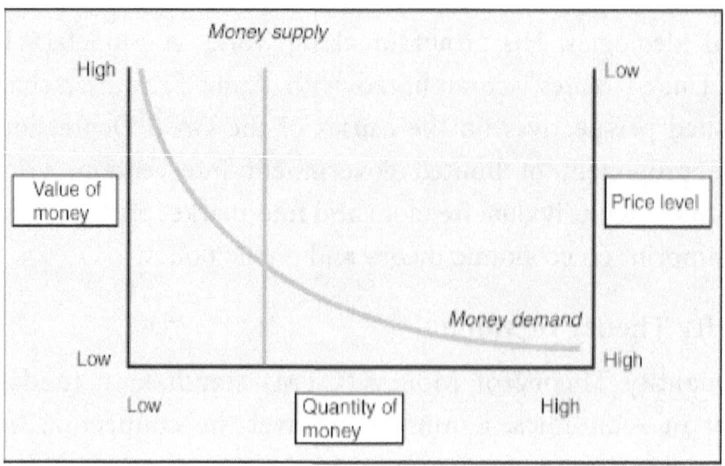

One key assumption of the Quantity Theory of Money is that changes in the money supply lead to proportional changes in the price level, expressed as the equation $M * V = P * T$. This assumption forms the basis for understanding inflation. If the money supply increases while the velocity of money and the volume of transactions remain constant, prices are expected to rise. Conversely, a decrease in the money supply may result in deflation.

The velocity of money represents the speed at which money circulates in the economy and is influenced by factors such as consumer spending habits, banking practices, and technological advancements. Critics argue that velocity is not constant and can fluctuate, challenging the simplicity of the theory. In response, economists have developed alternative versions, such as the Cambridge cash-balance approach, which considers money demand.

The Quantity Theory of Money has played a significant role in shaping discussions on monetary policy. Central banks, striving for stable prices and economic growth, often use the theory as a guide for adjusting interest rates and controlling the money supply. The equation of exchange, $MV = PT$, has been pivotal in formulating macroeconomic models and understanding the interplay between money and prices.

Practically, the Quantity Theory of Money has been applied to analyse historical episodes of hyperinflation and monetary policy decisions. For instance, during the hyperinflationary period in Weimar Germany in the early 1920s, the massive increase in the money supply led to a corresponding surge in prices, aligning with the theory's predictions. Similarly, the monetarist experiments of the 1980s, such as those in the United States under Chairman Paul Volcker, aimed at controlling inflation by targeting the money supply growth.

Despite its historical significance, the Quantity Theory of Money has faced challenges and refinements. Modern macroeconomic models, including the Keynesian revolution and subsequent New Keynesian approaches, introduced nuances and complexities that questioned the simplicity of the original theory. Keynesians emphasised the role of aggregate demand and rejected the idea of a stable velocity of money.

A key debate revolves around the transmission mechanism through which changes in the money supply affect the economy. While the theory establishes a clear relationship between money and prices, the pathway by which these changes influence real output and employment remains a subject of ongoing discussion. Keynesians argue that changes in the money supply can impact spending, output, and employment through various channels, including interest rates and expectations.

In recent decades, the Quantity Theory of Money has seen a revival of interest as researchers explore its applicability in different economic environments. The advent of new monetary aggregates and financial innovations has prompted economists to revisit the theory's assumptions and consider its relevance in the context of a dynamic and evolving financial system.

BOND ANALYSIS

First, let's get the definition out of the way.

The Cambridge Dictionary defines bonds as "an official paper given by the government or a company to show that you have lent them money that they will pay back to you at a particular interest rate."

ROLE OF BONDS IN FINANCIAL MARKETS

1. Capital Formation: Bonds play a crucial role in the journey of capital formation, serving as a key avenue through which governments, corporations, and municipalities gather financial resources for diverse needs. Governments often turn to bonds to bankroll public infrastructure projects, address budget shortfalls, or navigate economic downturns. Likewise, corporations issue bonds to support endeavours like expansions, research and development, or restructuring existing debt. Municipalities also tap into bonds to secure funds for local initiatives such as schools, hospitals, and public utilities. In essence, the bond market serves as a vital platform, enabling a wide range of entities to access capital from a diverse investor base, thereby fostering economic growth and development.

2. Diversification:

a. Risk Management: Diversification stands out as a fundamental principle in the prudent handling of risk. Bonds, distinguished by their typically lower volatility in comparison to equities, serve as a valuable instrument for investors seeking to fortify risk management within their portfolios. By integrating bonds alongside more unpredictable assets, such as stocks, one can effectively balance the overall risk profile of an investment portfolio. The distinct performance dynamics of bonds, influenced by factors divergent from equities, yield a portfolio less vulnerable to extreme price movements and market uncertainties.

b. Statistical Correlation: Bonds frequently exhibit a lower correlation with stocks, and in certain instances, may even demonstrate a negative correlation, particularly during periods of economic strain. This implies that during equity downturns, bonds can act as a counterbalance by either maintaining their value or undergoing less severe price declines. The non-correlated or negatively correlated nature of bonds renders them a potent tool for diminishing overall portfolio risk, providing investors with a smoother journey through diverse market conditions.

c. Stability/Reliability: While stocks may offer capital appreciation, they often fall short of providing a reliable and predictable income source. Bonds, in contrast, generate regular interest payments, offering a predictable cash flow. This income stability is particularly advantageous for investors reliant on portfolio income for living expenses, such as retirees. The amalgamation of income-generating bonds with other asset classes forges a more balanced portfolio addressing both capital appreciation and income generation objectives.

d. Duration Matching: In the world of investing for institutions, where meeting financial responsibilities over the long haul is crucial, strategies like duration matching and liability-driven investing (LDI) play a key role. These approaches are especially important for entities like pension funds and insurance companies, responsible for handling assets to fulfil future obligations such as pension payments or insurance claims.

So, what's duration matching all about? It's basically aligning the durations of your assets with your liabilities. Duration here reflects how sensitive an investment is to changes in interest rates. Bonds, being financial instruments with set maturities, have a duration corresponding to when they'll be repaid. By smartly matching the durations of bonds in a portfolio with expected payout obligations or liabilities, institutions can lessen the impact of interest rate changes on their financial well-being.

Now, let's dive into Liability-Driven Investing (LDI). It goes beyond duration matching and aims to manage risks tied to meeting future obligations, focusing on specific liabilities an institution has. This means constructing an investment portfolio that considers cash flows and durations of liabilities. The main goal is to make sure assets are in a good position to meet those liabilities when they're due. Take pension funds, for instance. With a predictable schedule of future pension payments to retirees, duration matching becomes super important. By holding bonds with maturities that align with expected payout obligations, pension funds can lower exposure to interest rate risk. When interest rates go up, longer-maturity bonds might see prices drop, but this is balanced out by the increased income from higher-yielding bonds.

TYPES OF BONDS

1. Government Bonds: Government bonds are essentially IOUs issued by national governments to raise funds for public spending. They're regarded as one of the safest bets in the financial world, backed by the government's taxing authority. When you invest in government bonds, you're essentially lending money to the government, and in return, you receive regular interest payments along with the return of the principal amount when the bond matures.

These bonds are a big deal in financial markets because they set a standard for interest rates. When things get shaky or uncertain in the economy, investors often turn to government bonds for their stability. In the U.S., we have Treasury Bonds, the U.K. has Gilts, and Germany has Bunds.

So, what makes government bonds tick? They offer relatively low yields compared to riskier investments, but they make up for it with their safety and easy convertibility to cash. This makes them attractive to conservative investors or those looking for a safe harbour during market storms. Many people use government bonds to diversify their investment portfolios and create a solid foundation for a balanced strategy.

2. Corporate Bonds: Corporate bonds operate as a form of financial agreement where companies issue debt securities to secure funds for diverse business purposes, such as expanding operations, funding research and development, or refinancing existing debts. When individuals invest in corporate bonds, they are essentially providing a financial loan to the issuing corporation. In return, investors receive periodic interest payments and the repayment of the principal amount upon the bond's maturity.

Now, these bonds have a risk factor, and it depends on how financially stable the company is. Credit rating agencies like Moody's, Standard & Poor's, and Fitch help investors figure out this risk. Bonds with high ratings are seen as safe bets with lower returns, while those with lower ratings, often called high-yield or junk bonds, can give you more returns but come with a higher chance of the company defaulting.

Investors in corporate bonds have to deal with two main types of risks. First, there's interest rate risk – basically, changes in market interest rates can affect the value of existing bonds. Then there's credit risk, which is about the company being able to meet its debt obligations. Economic downturns, industry-specific problems, or financial mismanagement can make this risk go up.

Corporate bonds can be more rewarding than government bonds, but they also come with more risk. That's why many investors mix things up, holding a variety of both government and corporate bonds based on how much risk they're comfortable with and what they're aiming for. In times when the economy is doing well, corporate bonds might do better than government ones because companies are thriving, making them more reliable.

3. HYB/Junk Bonds: High-yield bonds, commonly referred to as "junk bonds," constitute a distinctive segment within the fixed-income market, distinguished by elevated risk and correspondingly heightened potential returns. Issued by entities with credit ratings falling below investment-grade, typically rated Ba1/BB+ (we will talk more about credit ratings in the future) or lower by esteemed agencies such as Moody's and Standard & Poor's, these debt securities are characterised by their capacity to offer investors enhanced yields relative to their investment-grade counterparts. Nevertheless, the allure of augmented yield is accompanied by a commensurate increase in the risk of default.

Investing in high-yield bonds necessitates navigating a landscape where credit risk assumes paramount significance. Issuing entities are often characterised by weakened financial positions, stemming from factors such as business models, industry dynamics, or unique circumstances. Consequently, the yields on high-yield bonds serve as compensation to investors for the heightened risk of potential defaults—a risk subject to dynamism influenced by economic conditions, industry trends, and the financial health of individual issuers.

Market dynamics play a pivotal role in the performance of high-yield bonds. Economic upswings may render these bonds attractive, as companies experience improved profitability. Conversely, economic downturns amplify the risk of default, consequently impacting the valuation of high-yield bonds. Investors in this asset class are well-advised to closely monitor economic indicators and remain attuned to shifts in market sentiment.

High-yield bonds span a spectrum of sectors and industries, encompassing technology, healthcare, energy, and consumer goods. Each sector introduces its own set of risks and opportunities, obliging investors to carefully consider industry-specific factors that may exert influence on the creditworthiness of issuers. For instance, energy companies may contend with challenges related to commodity price fluctuations, thereby affecting their capacity to service debt.

BOND FEATURES

Face Value and Par Value

Think of face value as the official sticker price or declared worth of a financial security, like a bond. It's what the issuer says the security is worth. For bonds, this figure represents the amount the bond will be worth when it matures, and it's usually what the bondholder gets back at that time.

Par value is pretty much the same as face value—it's the amount a bond is initially sold for or can be redeemed for by the issuer when it matures. Bonds are typically issued with a par value of $1,000, and that's what the bondholder gets back when the bond reaches its maturity date. But, keep in mind, the actual market price of a bond might be different due to changes in interest rates and how risky people think it is.

Coupon Rate:

The coupon rate is the fixed yearly interest rate that a bond promises to pay to the person holding the bond. It's a percentage of the face value. So, for instance, if a bond has a face value of $1,000 and a coupon rate of 5%, it means the bondholder gets $50 in interest each year. This fixed-rate feature sets it apart from bonds with changing interest rates.

These regular coupon payments provide a steady income for bondholders, making fixed-income securities appealing to those who want consistent returns. The coupon rates are set when the bond is first sold and stay the same throughout its life, regardless of changes in wider interest rates. This predictability makes bonds an important part of portfolios for people looking for steady income.

Maturity Date:

The maturity date is when the main payment happens for bondholders. It's when the principal amount is returned. This date marks the end of a bond's life. Maturity dates are set when the bond is first sold and can range from a few months to several decades later. Short-term bonds mature quickly, giving investors faster access to their money, while long-term bonds provide income over a longer period but might mean tying up funds for an extended time.

When putting together an investment portfolio, investors consider maturity dates to match up with their goals and investment horizon. Matching bond maturities with financial goals helps manage the need for liquidity and the investor's risk tolerance.

Yield to Maturity (YTM):

*Yield to Maturity (YTM) provides a complete picture of what an investor can expect from a bond if held until maturity. It takes into account the current market price of the bond, the coupon interest rate, and the time remaining until the maturity date. YTM is expressed as an annual percentage rate (APR). It considers the interest income and any gain or loss on the bond if held until maturity.

CREDIT RATING

Let's talk about some types of risk.

Default Risk:

Understanding default risk, also referred to as credit risk, is crucial in the analysis of bonds. It represents the likelihood that an issuer may face challenges in meeting its debt obligations. This factor plays a pivotal role in shaping bond pricing and significantly influences the decisions made by discerning investors.

To grasp the intricacies of default risk, a comprehensive examination is necessary. This involves combining insights into the financial well-being of the issuer, the dynamics of its industry, and broader economic conditions. At its essence, default risk encompasses the potential non-payment of interest and principal by the bond issuer. Investors, aware of this inherent risk, seek compensation, which is reflected in the yield offered by the bond. To fully understand default risk, it is important to consider several key factors.

Credit Spread:

Credit spreads serve as an indicator of the compensation investors seek for shouldering credit risk. Essentially, they represent the difference between the yield on a riskier bond, like corporate bonds, and a comparable risk-free instrument. Credit spreads offer valuable insights into market perceptions of credit risk and prevailing economic conditions.

To calculate and interpret credit spreads, one subtracts the yield on a corporate bond from the yield on a government bond with a similar maturity. The resulting spread reflects the extra yield demanded by investors for holding a bond that carries credit risk. A widening spread suggests growing credit concerns, while a narrowing spread indicates an improvement in credit conditions.

Market sentiment, a volatile force in financial markets, plays a significant role in influencing credit spreads. During periods of economic uncertainty or financial stress, risk-averse investors often trigger wider credit spreads. Conversely, in favourable economic conditions, credit spreads may contract as investors seek higher-yielding assets.

Positive economic data tends to contribute to tighter spreads, indicating confidence in the creditworthiness of issuers. Changes in interest rates, particularly those influenced by central bank actions, can impact the cost of borrowing and, consequently, influence credit spreads.

Credit Default Swaps (Case Study Provided):

A credit default swap operates as a bilateral agreement between two parties, the protection buyer and the protection seller. The protection buyer essentially seeks insurance against the risk of default or other credit events associated with a specific reference entity. This reference entity can vary widely and might include corporations, government entities, or even baskets of assets such as mortgage-backed securities.

The protection buyer, in exchange for this coverage, pays a periodic premium to the protection seller.

The premium payments are akin to insurance premiums and are usually expressed as a percentage of the notional amount, which is the face value of the reference entity's debt. It's crucial to note that the protection buyer does not necessarily need to own any of the underlying debt of the reference entity. This aspect makes CDS distinct from traditional insurance, where the policyholder typically owns the underlying asset being insured.

The protection seller, on the other hand, assumes the risk of the credit event occurring. In the event of a credit event, such as default, bankruptcy, or a debt restructuring, the protection seller is obligated to compensate the protection buyer. The compensation is typically the face value of the debt, although the exact terms may be negotiated in the CDS contract.

Credit default swaps are customisable financial instruments, allowing parties to tailor the terms of the contract to their specific needs. This includes specifying the trigger events that would lead to a payout, defining the notional amount, and determining the duration of the contract. The flexibility and customisation of CDS contracts make them valuable tools for a variety of risk management strategies.

One of the primary uses of credit default swaps is hedging against credit risk. Investors and financial institutions can use CDS to protect themselves from potential losses arising from adverse credit events. For example, if an investor holds a portfolio of bonds and wants to hedge against the risk of default in one of those bonds, they can enter into a CDS contract on that specific bond.

However, CDS are not exclusively used for hedging purposes. They are also employed for speculative purposes, where investors take positions on the creditworthiness of a particular entity without necessarily owning its debt. This speculative aspect has been a source of controversy, as it introduces an element of risk that extends beyond the traditional bounds of the underlying assets.

2007–2008 CRISIS

The 2007–2008 financial crisis had its roots in the U.S. housing market, specifically the subprime mortgage sector. Financial institutions created complex securities, such as mortgage-backed securities (MBS) and collateralised debt obligations (CDOs), by bundling subprime mortgages. As housing prices declined and subprime borrowers began to default on their mortgages, the value of these securities plummeted. This triggered a chain reaction of financial distress.

Credit default swaps (CDS) played a pivotal role in the crisis through their use as both risk management tools and speculative instruments. Financial institutions and investors used CDS to hedge against the default risk associated with MBS and CDOs. However, the sheer volume and complexity of these derivatives led to a lack of transparency. Investors often held CDS on assets they did not own, creating a disconnect between the parties exposed to the underlying risk and those managing it through CDS.

Consequently, as the housing market collapsed, the interconnectedness of financial institutions became evident. Institutions holding mortgage-related assets faced significant losses, triggering the need to pay out on CDS contracts. The domino effect was exacerbated by the speculative use of CDS, as some entities had taken large, leveraged positions betting against mortgage-backed securities. When these bets went awry, massive losses were incurred, contributing to the crisis.

The bankruptcy of Lehman Brothers in September 2008 is a pivotal event in the crisis and exemplifies the consequences of the CDS market. Lehman Brothers, heavily involved in the CDS market, had substantial exposure to mortgage-backed securities. As it faced insolvency, the interconnected nature of CDS contracts became evident, leading to a loss of confidence in the financial system. The bankruptcy triggered a freeze in credit markets as uncertainty spread regarding the exposure of other financial institutions to CDS and mortgage-related assets.

The consequences of the crisis were severe and far-reaching. Major financial institutions faced insolvency, requiring government interventions and bailouts to prevent a complete collapse of the financial system. The crisis led to a global recession, causing widespread unemployment, foreclosures, and economic hardships. Regulatory responses were implemented to address the systemic risks associated with derivatives, including increased scrutiny of the CDS market and efforts to enhance transparency and risk management practices. The 2007–2008 financial crisis underscored the need for vigilant oversight and risk mitigation in financial markets, especially in the realm of complex financial instruments like credit default swaps.

RECOVERY RATES

Recovery rate signifies the proportion of a bond's face value that creditors can recoup in the event of a default by the issuer. In essence, it serves as a measure of the potential losses creditors may incur in such an adverse scenario. The recovery rate is expressed as a percentage and is determined by the liquidation value of the defaulted assets, often realised through bankruptcy proceedings or restructuring efforts.

One must distinguish the recovery rate from the concept of face value or par value, which represents the nominal value of the bond. In the aftermath of a default, bondholders may not receive the entire face value of the bond. Instead, the recovery rate encapsulates the percentage of the initial investment that creditors can salvage. For example, if a bond has a face value of $1,000 and the recovery rate is 60%, creditors would expect to recover $600 in the event of a default.

Recovery Rate = (Actual amount recovered / face value of bond) * 100

Several factors influence the determination of recovery rates. Chief among these is the collateral securing the bond. Secured bonds, backed by specific assets, tend to have higher recovery rates as these assets can be liquidated to satisfy creditor claims. Unsecured bonds, lacking such collateral, often have lower recovery rates, exposing creditors to greater potential losses.

CREDIT RISK MODELS

We will talk about two different models.

Merton Model

The Merton Model, developed by Robert C. Merton in the early 1970s, is a structural credit risk model that provides a framework for assessing the credit risk of a firm by modelling the relationship between the firm's assets and liabilities. This model is grounded in the idea that a company can be viewed as a portfolio of assets. The underlying assumption is that if the value of the firm's assets falls below a certain threshold (the face value of its debt), default occurs, and the debt holders take control of the firm.

The key components of the Merton Model include the firm's asset value, the amount of debt, the volatility of the firm's assets, and the risk-free rate. The model assumes that the value of the firm's assets follows a geometric Brownian (random) motion, capturing the random movements in asset values over time. The volatility of the assets reflects the uncertainty or risk associated with these movements. The Merton

Model produces an estimate of the probability of default (PD), which represents the likelihood that the firm will be unable to meet its debt obligations.

Credit Scoring Model

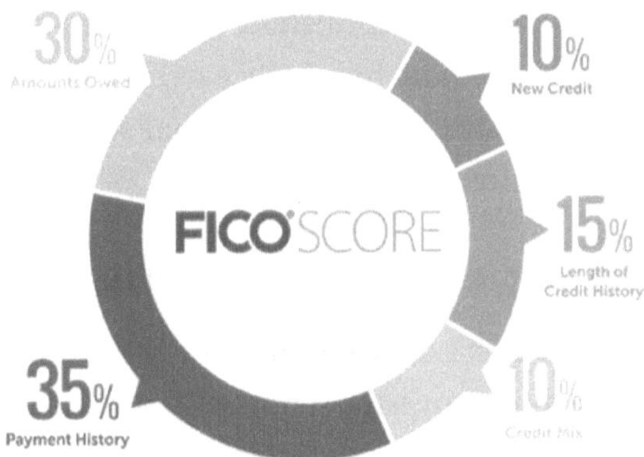

A Credit Scoring Model is a sophisticated statistical tool designed to comprehensively assess the creditworthiness of individuals or businesses by analysing various financial and non-financial factors. These models play an important role in predicting the likelihood of a borrower defaulting on a loan or failing to meet credit obligations. One of the primary components, Payment History, holds the most significant weight (35%) and scrutinises an individual's track record in meeting payment deadlines, encompassing considerations such as late payments, defaults, and bankruptcies. Credit Utilisation (30%) evaluates the ratio of current credit card balances to credit limits, with lower utilisation signalling favourable credit management. Length of Credit History (15%) considers the duration of active credit accounts, favouring longer histories for their predictability. Types of Credit in Use (10%) assesses the diversity of credit accounts, reflecting positively on individuals managing different types responsibly. New Credit (10%) examines recent credit activities, emphasising the potential impact of multiple new accounts on credit risk.

Credit scores typically range from 300 to 850, with higher scores indicating lower credit risk. These scores undergo rigorous development, validation, and continuous monitoring to ensure accuracy and regulatory compliance. Lenders often customise these models, integrating credit scores into decision systems for efficient and objective lending practices. Continuous updates and potential integration of alternative data contribute to fair and transparent credit assessment. Examples include the widely used FICO Score and Vantage Score, with some industries adopting specialised models tailored to specific risk considerations.

ECONOMIC INDICATORS AND BONDS

Economic indicators exert a profound influence on the dynamics of the bond market, shaping investor sentiment and impacting the pricing and yields of bonds. One of the most critical factors is the movement of interest rates. Bonds exhibit an inverse relationship with interest rates, whereby rising rates tend to depress bond prices, as existing bonds with lower coupon rates become less attractive compared to new issuances in a higher-rate environment. Central banks, notably the Federal Reserve in the U.S., wield significant influence over short-term interest rates, making their policy decisions closely watched by bond investors.

Inflation rates represent another crucial factor affecting bonds. Inflation erodes the real return on fixed-income investments, prompting investors to demand higher yields to offset the anticipated loss in purchasing power. Bond markets react sensitively to inflation data, and unexpected changes in inflation rates can lead to heightened volatility.

The health of the overall economy, as measured by the Gross Domestic Product (GDP), plays a pivotal role in shaping bond market dynamics. Robust GDP growth may signal higher inflation and, subsequently, higher interest rates, impacting the value of existing bonds. Similarly, employment and unemployment rates are closely scrutinised by bond investors. Low unemployment and robust job creation may contribute to inflationary pressures, influencing expectations for future interest rate movements.

Indices like the Consumer Price Index (CPI) and Producer Price Index (PPI) serve as vital indicators of inflationary pressures. Bond investors carefully monitor these indices for signs of rising prices, which can impact both short- and long-term interest rates. Additionally, the statements and policy decisions of central banks, such as the Federal Reserve, hold substantial sway over the bond market. Clarity or hints about future monetary policy directions can trigger significant movements in bond prices.

Government fiscal policy is yet another determinant, as spending and taxation policies influence economic growth and inflation. Fiscal stimulus measures or austerity policies can impact interest rates and subsequently affect the bond market. Economic conditions in major economies worldwide can influence investor sentiment and contribute to global interest rate trends, prompting investors to diversify their bond portfolios in response to international economic developments.

YIELD CURVE ANALYSIS

Let's first look at the types of Yield Curves.

THE YIELD CURVE

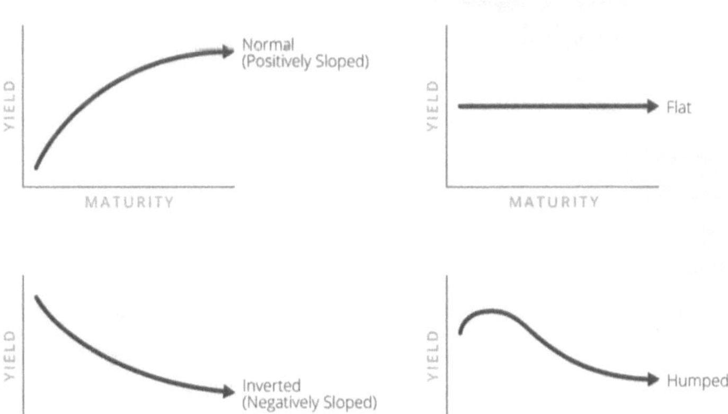

1. Normal Yield Curve

A normal yield curve is characterised by upward-sloping lines, indicating that long-term interest rates are higher than short-term rates. This is the most common shape and is associated with expectations of economic expansion. Investors demand higher compensation for the increased risk and time associated with longer-term investments. In a healthy economic environment, the normal yield curve reflects the anticipation of future growth and higher inflation.

2. Inverted Yield Curve

An inverted yield curve occurs when short-term interest rates are higher than long-term rates, resulting in a downward-sloping curve. This phenomenon is often considered a harbinger of economic downturns. Investors accepting lower long-term yields may be signalling concerns about the economy, anticipating lower interest rates in the future. Historically, an inverted yield curve has preceded recessions, making it a closely watched indicator by investors and economists.

3. Flat Yield Curve

A flat yield curve is characterised by minimal differences between short-term and long-term interest rates, resulting in a nearly horizontal line. This shape often emerges during transitional periods in the economy, reflecting uncertainty about future interest rate movements. Investors may perceive limited prospects for economic growth or inflation. While a flat yield curve does not necessarily predict a recession, it can indicate a cautious market sentiment.

4. Humped Yield Curve

A humped yield curve, as the name suggests, features a slight rise in the middle maturity ranges, creating a curve that resembles a hill or hump. This shape may suggest uncertainty about the direction of future interest rates. The short-term rates on one side of the hump may be influenced by current economic conditions, while long-term rates on the other side reflect expectations for the future. The humped yield curve is less common but underscores the complexities of market sentiment.

EXPECTATIONS THEORY

The Expectations Theory, a fundamental concept in financial economics, delves into the intricate relationship between short-term and long-term interest rates, offering insights into how the yield curve evolves over time. At its core, the theory says that the shape of the yield curve reflects investors' expectations regarding the future path of short-term interest rates. According to this theory, the interest rate on a long-term bond is envisioned as the average of the short-term interest rates expected by investors throughout the bond's tenure. This implies that the yield curve's configuration is primarily influenced by the collective anticipations of market participants regarding the trajectory of future short-term rates.

The Pure Expectations Hypothesis, a specific form of the Expectations Theory, refines this concept by proposing that the yield on a long-term bond serves as an unbiased predictor of future short-term interest rates. In simpler terms, the yield curve shape is exclusively determined by the consensus expectations for future short-term rates. Practical applications involve the calculation of forward rates, representing the expected future interest rates implied by the prevailing yield curve. These forward rates aid investors in assessing the anticipated trajectory of interest rates over specific future periods.

While the Expectations Theory provides a valuable framework for interpreting the yield curve, its application is contingent upon certain assumptions. The theory presupposes that investors are risk-neutral, making decisions solely based on expectations of future interest rates.

LIQUIDITY PREFERENCE THEORY

The Liquidity Preference Theory, developed by John Maynard Keynes, provides a comprehensive explanation for the term structure of interest rates. At its core, the Liquidity Preference Theory asserts that investors require a premium for holding longer-term securities due to the added risk and uncertainty associated with tying up funds for an extended period.

Keynes identified three motives for holding money: the transaction motive, precautionary motive, and speculative motive. The speculative motive is particularly relevant to the Liquidity Preference Theory. According to this motive, investors prefer holding money over longer-term bonds when they anticipate changes in interest rates. If interest rates are expected to rise, investors prefer the flexibility of holding cash or short-term securities to take advantage of higher rates in the future.

The theory further distinguishes between the liquidity of money and the illiquidity of long-term bonds. Money, in the form of cash or short-term securities, is highly liquid, meaning it can be quickly and easily converted into goods or services. In contrast, long-term bonds, with fixed interest rates, are less liquid because selling them before maturity involves the risk of capital loss due to changes in interest rates.

As interest rates rise, the opportunity cost of holding money increases, and investors become more willing to lock in higher yields by investing in longer-term bonds. Conversely, when interest rates are expected to fall or remain low, investors may prefer the liquidity of short-term assets.

The Liquidity Preference Theory contends that the term structure of interest rates reflects the interplay between the demand for liquidity and the supply of funds available for investment. The theory posits that long-term interest rates comprise a series of short-term interest rates plus a premium for the added risk and illiquidity associated with holding longer-term assets.

MARKET SEGMENTATION THEORY

Market Segmentation Theory is a fundamental concept in the field of fixed-income securities and interest rate analysis, offering insights into the behaviour of bond investors and the dynamics of the yield curve. Proposed as an alternative to the Expectations Theory and Liquidity

Preference Theory, Market Segmentation Theory suggests that the bond market is segmented into distinct maturity segments, and investors have specific preferences and demands for bonds of different maturities.

According to Market Segmentation Theory, investors have particular investment horizons and preferences for the term structure of interest rates. These preferences lead to the segmentation of the bond market into different maturity sectors, such as short-term, intermediate-term, and long-term bonds. Investors choose bonds that align with their investment time horizons, creating relatively independent markets for each maturity segment.

One key implication of Market Segmentation Theory is that changes in interest rates for one maturity segment do not necessarily impact rates in other segments. In other words, the yields on short-term bonds are determined by supply and demand factors specific to the short-term market, without direct influence from expectations about future short-term rates or long-term rates. This contrasts with the Expectations Theory, which posits a connection between short-term and long-term rates based on market expectations.

The theory also implies that the shape of the yield curve is a result of the supply and demand dynamics within each maturity segment rather than a reflection of expectations about future interest rates. For instance, if there is increased demand for long-term bonds due to a preference for safety and stability, the yield curve may become downward-sloping (inverted) even if investors do not anticipate lower future short-term rates.

Market Segmentation Theory acknowledges that investors may be influenced by factors such as risk aversion, investment policies, and regulatory constraints, leading them to focus on specific segments of the yield curve. This segmentation creates distinct markets for various maturities, and changes in interest rates within one segment are primarily driven by factors specific to that segment.

Bond Rating

Rating	Moody's	Standard & Poor's	Fitch
AAA	Highest quality, lowest credit risk.	Extremely strong capacity to meet financial commitments	Exceptionally strong capacity for payment of financial commitments
AA	High quality, very low credit risk	Very strong capacity to meet financial commitments	Very high capacity for payment
A	Upper-medium quality, low credit risk	Strong capacity to meet financial commitments	High capacity for payment
BAA/BBB	Medium quality, moderate credit risk	Adequate capacity to meet financial commitments	Good capacity for payment
BA/BB	Speculative, substantial credit risk	Less vulnerable in the near term but faces major ongoing uncertainties	Speculative, indicating a higher level of vulnerability to default
B	Highly speculative, high credit risk	More vulnerable to adverse business, financial, and economic conditions	Highly speculative with a potential for default
CAA/CCC	Poor standing, very high credit risk	Currently vulnerable, and is dependent upon favourable business, financial, and economic conditions to meet financial commitments	Substantial credit risk

CA/CC	Highly speculative with a likelihood of default	Currently highly vulnerable	Very high levels of credit risk
C	Lowest rated, typically in default or near default	Currently highly vulnerable to nonpayment, and is dependent upon favourable business, financial, and economic conditions to meet financial commitments	Default is imminent
RD	----	----	Restricted default
D	----	In default on financial commitments	Default

FINANCIAL STATEMENTS

Understanding how to invest wisely requires getting a grip on where your money is going. That's where financial statement analysis comes into play. Think of it as a detailed magnifying glass that lets investors zoom in on a company's financial health. The income statement, balance sheet, and cash flow statement—all these documents paint a picture of how well a company is doing.

By digging into these financial reports, investors can figure out if a company is making money, managing debts, and staying afloat. This analysis isn't just about the past; it's a tool to predict a company's future. Investors can spot trends and make educated guesses about where a company is headed.

Financial statement analysis also makes it easier to compare companies in the same industry. It helps investors find those with the best financial health and growth potential. In the risky world of investing, being able to read financial statements is like having a secret weapon. It helps investors make smarter choices, understand and handle risks, and keep their investment strategies in line with their money goals. So, let's dive into the basics of financial statement analysis—a crucial skill for anyone looking to make sense of the investment game.

INCOME STATEMENT

The income statement, also known as the profit and loss (P&L) statement or statement of earnings, is a financial document that provides a summary of a company's revenues, expenses, gains, and losses during a specific period, typically a quarter or a year. Its primary purpose is to offer stakeholders a comprehensive view of a company's financial performance, revealing whether the business is generating a profit or incurring losses.

The income statement is divided into several components, each shedding light on different aspects of a company's financial activities. At the top line, we find revenues (total net sales), which encompass all the money earned through the core operations of the business. This includes sales of goods or services, interest, and any other income generated from primary business activities. Deducted from revenues are various expenses, such as the cost of goods sold (COGS), operating expenses, interest, and taxes. The result is the operating income, a key indicator of the profitability derived directly from the core operations of the business.

Beyond operating items, the income statement also captures gains and losses from non-operating activities. Non-operating items may include gains or losses from the sale of assets, investments, or other extraordinary events outside the company's regular operations. The inclusion of these non-operating items allows stakeholders to understand the full scope of a company's financial performance, beyond its day-to-day activities.

One crucial concept within the income statement is net income, which represents the company's overall profitability. Net income is calculated by subtracting all expenses, including operating and non-operating items, from the total revenues. A positive net income indicates a profit, while a negative net income signals a loss. This bottom-line figure is instrumental for investors, analysts, and management in assessing the financial health and sustainability of the business.

Sample Products Co.
Income Statement
For the Five Months Ended May 31, 2017

Sales		$100,000
Cost of goods sold		75,000
Gross profit		25,000
Operating expenses		
Selling expenses		
Advertising expense	2,000	
Commissions expense	5,000	7,000
Administrative expenses		
Office supplies expense	3,500	
Office equipment expense	2,500	6,000
Total operating expenses		13,000
Operating income		12,000
Non-Operating or other		
Interest revenues		5,000
Gain on sale of investments		3,000
Interest expense		(500)
Loss from lawsuit		(1,500)
Total non-operating		6,000
Net Income		$ 18,000

BALANCE SHEET

The balance sheet, a key financial statement, provides a snapshot of a company's financial position at a specific point in time. It breaks down the company's economic resources and obligations into three main categories: assets, liabilities, and equity.

Assets:

Assets represent what the company owns, and they are further categorised into current and non-current assets. Current assets are those expected to be converted into cash or used up within a year. This includes cash and cash equivalents, accounts receivable (amounts owed by customers), and inventory. These items are considered short-term holdings, providing insight into a company's liquidity and its ability to meet immediate financial obligations. Non-current assets, on the other hand, encompass long-term investments, property, and equipment. These are assets with a longer useful life, contributing to a company's overall value and operational capacity.

Liabilities:

Liabilities denote the company's obligations, and like assets, they are divided into current and non-current liabilities. Current liabilities encompass obligations expected to be settled within a year, such as accounts payable (amounts owed to suppliers) and short-term debt. This provides a snapshot of the company's short-term financial obligations. Non-current liabilities, including long-term debts and obligations, extend beyond the one-year horizon. Analysing these liabilities offers insights into the company's long-term financial commitments and its ability to manage them over time.

Equity:

Equity represents the residual interest of the owners in the company after deducting liabilities from assets. It's essentially the net assets attributable to the company's shareholders. Equity is a measure of the company's net worth and is crucial for understanding the ownership structure. When liabilities are subtracted from assets, the remainder is the shareholders' equity. This equity is the owners' stake in the company, signifying their claim on its assets after all obligations have been settled. It serves as an indicator of the company's financial health and attractiveness to potential investors.

At the core of the balance sheet is the accounting equation:

Assets = Liabilities + Equity

This equation is a fundamental principle in accounting, ensuring a consistent balance between a company's resources and its obligations.

The significance of the balance sheet is evident in its role in assessing a company's solvency and liquidity. Solvency is evaluated by considering the proportion of a company's assets that can cover its long-term obligations, indicating its ability to meet long-term debt commitments. Liquidity, meanwhile, is assessed by comparing current assets to current liabilities, revealing the company's capacity to meet short-term obligations. These metrics are vital for investors and analysts, providing insights into a company's financial stability and risk.

Sample Balance Sheet

Example Corporation
Balance Sheet
December 31, 2022

ASSETS		LIABILITIES	
Current assets		**Current liabilities**	
Cash and cash equivalents	$ 2,200	Short-term loans payable	$ 5,000
Short-term investments	10,000	Current portion of long-term debt	15,000
Accounts receivable - net	39,500	Accounts payable	20,900
Other receivables	1,000	Accrued compensation and benefits	8,500
Inventory	31,000	Income taxes payable	6,100
Supplies	3,800	Other accrued liabilities	4,000
Prepaid expenses	1,500	Deferred revenues	1,500
Total current assets	89,000	Total current liabilities	61,000
Investments	36,000	**Long-term liabilities**	
		Notes payable	20,000
Property, plant & equipment - net		Bonds payable	375,000
Land	5,500	Deferred income taxes	25,000
Land improvements	6,500	Total long-term liabilities	420,000
Buildings	180,000		
Equipment	201,000	Total liabilities	481,000
Less: accumulated depreciation	(56,000)		
Property, plant & equipment - net	337,000	Commitments and contingencies (see notes)	
Intangible assets	.	STOCKHOLDERS' EQUITY	
Goodwill	105,000		
Other intangible assets	200,000	Common stock	110,000
Total intangible assets	305,000	Retained earnings	220,000
		Accum other comprehensive income	9,000
Other assets	3,000	Less: Treasury stock	(50,000)
		Total stockholders' equity	289,000
Total assets	$ 770,000	Total liabilities & stockholders' equity	$ 770,000

The accompanying notes are an integral part of this statement.

CASH FLOW STATEMENT

1. Operating Activities:

This section constitutes the core operational aspects of a business. It encompasses cash transactions related to day-to-day activities, such as sales, purchases of inventory, payment of wages, and settlement of operating expenses. A positive cash flow from operating activities signifies that the company is generating cash through its primary business operations. It also accounts for adjustments like depreciation, changes in working capital, and non-cash items, providing a comprehensive representation of the actual cash generated.

2. Investing Activities:

The investing activities section focuses on the acquisition and disposition of long-term assets. Capital expenditures, purchases or sales of property and equipment, and investments in securities fall under this category. A positive cash flow in this section may indicate strategic investments for future growth, while negative cash flow might suggest divestment or asset liquidation.

3. Financing Activities:

Financing activities involve transactions with a company's owners and creditors. Issuing or repurchasing stocks, obtaining or repaying loans, and paying dividends are recorded in this section. Positive cash flow here may denote external funding or shareholder returns, while negative cash flow may signify debt repayment or stock buybacks.

Cash Flow from Operating Activities vs. Net Income:

Understanding the difference between cash flow from operating activities and net income is crucial. Net income represents the profit or loss recorded on the income statement, incorporating accrual-based accounting principles. In contrast, cash flow from operating activities adjusts for non-cash items and changes in working capital, offering a more realistic portrayal of a company's cash position. Discrepancies between the two metrics can unveil insights into the quality of earnings and the efficiency of cash management.

Importance in Evaluating a Company's Ability to Generate Cash:

The significance of the Cash Flow Statement lies in its role as a barometer of a company's cash-generating capacity. Positive cash flow indicates that a company can meet its operational expenses, pursue growth initiatives, and fulfil financial obligations. This is particularly crucial during economic downturns or challenging business environments, as positive cash flow serves as a buffer against unforeseen disruptions. On the other hand, persistent negative cash flow can raise red flags about a company's sustainability and may necessitate a closer examination of its financial strategies.

Table to compare and contrast

Aspect	Income Statement	Balance Sheet	Cash Flow Statement
Purpose	Summarises revenues and expenses to calculate net income or loss during a specific period.	Provides a snapshot of a company's financial position at a specific point in time.	Details the sources and uses of cash over a specific period, offering insights into a company's cash flow.
Time Frame	Covers a specific period, typically quarterly or annually.	Represents a single point in time, usually the end of a fiscal period.	Encompasses a specific period, often the same as the income statement, but can also be presented as a cumulative summary.
Focus	Focuses on the profitability of the business.	Focuses on the financial position of the business, including assets, liabilities, and equity.	Focuses on the cash movements within the business, detailing the sources and uses of cash.

Accrual VS Cash Basis	Primarily follows the accrual accounting method, recognising revenues and expenses when earned or incurred, not necessarily when cash changes hands.	A mix of accrual and cash methods. Assets and liabilities are recorded on an accrual basis, but some items may be reported on a cash basis.	Primarily follows the cash accounting method, recording transactions when cash is exchanged.
Net Income	Represents the company's profit or loss after deducting all expenses from revenue.	----	Included in the operating activities section but can differ from net income due to non-cash items and adjustments.
Financial Health Indicator	Provides insights into the profitability and operational efficiency of the business.	Indicates the overall financial health and liquidity position of the company.	Offers insights into a company's ability to generate cash, meet its obligations, and invest in future growth.

MANAGEMENT DISCUSSION AND ANALYSIS (MD&A)

Management Discussion and Analysis (MD&A) plays a crucial role in annual reports, acting as a vital link between the financial statements and the operational intricacies of a company. It serves as a comprehensive narrative carefully crafted by management to clarify the story behind the financial numbers and provide stakeholders with a detailed view of the company's performance and strategic direction.

The primary objective of MD&A is to offer stakeholders, including shareholders, investors, and analysts, a nuanced understanding of the company's financial performance during the reporting period. It serves as a platform for management to communicate the context, drivers, and implications behind the numerical data presented in the financial statements. This narrative interpretation is instrumental in turning raw financial figures into meaningful insights, facilitating a deeper comprehension of the company's overall health.

MD&A goes beyond the quantitative and delves into the qualitative aspects of a company's performance. It explains the strategic decisions, operational challenges, and successes that influenced the financial outcomes. By providing this context, management can present a more comprehensive perspective, enabling stakeholders to understand not just what happened but why it happened. For example, if there was a notable increase in expenses, MD&A would offer insights into the nature of these expenses, whether they were linked to strategic investments, operational expansions, or other factors.

RATIO ANALYSIS

A brief overview of some important ratios (Interpretations of each of these ratios is given in tabular format at the end of this section, for better understanding).

Current Ratio

The current ratio is a financial metric that measures a company's ability to cover its short-term obligations with its short-term assets. It is a liquidity ratio that helps assess a company's short-term financial health and its ability to meet its current liabilities using its current assets.

Current Ratio = Current Assets / Current Liabilities

Current Assets include cash, accounts receivable, inventory, and other assets that are expected to be converted into cash or used up within one year. Current Liabilities include obligations and debts that are due within one year, such as accounts payable, short-term loans, and other current liabilities.

Quick Ratio

The Quick Ratio, or Acid-Test Ratio, and the current ratio are both important financial metrics used to assess a company's liquidity, but they differ in their treatment of assets. The Quick Ratio is a more stringent measure as it excludes inventory from the calculation, focusing solely on the most liquid assets that can be rapidly converted into cash to meet short-term obligations. Components such as cash, short-term investments, and accounts receivable are considered, offering a conservative view of a company's immediate liquidity. On the other hand, the current ratio includes inventory in addition to other current assets, providing a broader perspective on overall liquidity.

Quick Ratio = (Cash & equivalents + Accounts receivable) / Current Liabilities

Accounts Receivable represents the money owed to the company by its customers for goods or services provided on credit.

Net Profit Margin (NPM)

The net profit margin is a critical indicator of a company's profitability. It measures the percentage of revenue that remains as net profit after deducting all expenses, including operating costs, interest, and taxes.

NPM = Net Income / Revenue

Gross Profit Margin

The gross profit margin assesses the profitability of a company's core business activities by examining the percentage of revenue remaining after deducting the direct costs associated with production. This includes materials, labour, and manufacturing expenses.

GPM = (Revenue – Cost of Goods Sold) / Revenue * 100

Operating Profit Margin

The operating profit margin zeros in on the profitability of a company's essential operations by assessing the percentage of revenue contributing to operating income. By excluding non-operating expenses like interest and taxes, it furnishes insights into the efficiency of day-to-day business activities.

OPM = (Revenue – Interest – Tax) / Net Sales * 100

Return on Asset

ROA probes into how proficiently a company leverages its assets to generate profit. It denotes the percentage of net income concerning the average total assets deployed during a specific period.

ROA = Net Income / Average Total Assets

Return on Equity

ROE gauges the yield generated for shareholders' equity, reflecting the company's ability to generate profits from the investments of shareholders.

ROE = Net Income / Shareholders' Equity

Return on Investment

ROI evaluates the profitability of an investment by contrasting the net profit with the entire cost of the investment. This metric provides insights into the return generated relative to the initial investment, aiding investors in gauging the success of their investment decisions.

ROI = Net Profit / Total Investment Cost

Earnings Before Interest and Taxes Margin (EBIT)

The EBIT margin concentrates on operational profitability by evaluating the percentage of revenue contributing to earnings before interest and taxes. By excluding non-operating expenses, it delivers a lucid depiction of the core profitability of the business and operational efficiency.

EBIT Margin = EBIT / Total Revenue

Earnings Before Interest, Taxes, Depreciation, and Amortisation (EBITDA) Margin

Analogous to the EBIT margin, the EBITDA margin sidesteps depreciation and amortisation. It offers a perspective on cash operating profitability, accentuating the company's ability to generate cash from core operations. EBITDA is especially pertinent in industries with substantial capital expenditures.

EBITDA Margin = EBITDA / Total Revenue

Profit Margin on Sales

The profit margin on sales quantifies the percentage of sales contributing to net profit. It offers a broad overview of overall profitability, taking into account all costs tied to producing and selling goods or services.

Profit Margin on Sales = Net Profit / Sales

Debt-to-Equity Ratio

The Debt-to-Equity Ratio evaluates how a company balances its use of debt and equity for financing. It offers insights into the firm's capital structure, revealing the degree to which it relies on borrowed funds versus shareholder investment. This ratio is crucial for assessing financial risk and understanding the potential impact on returns.

Debt-to-Equity Ratio = Total Debt / Shareholders' Equity

Debt Ratio

The debt ratio measures the proportion of a company's assets funded by debt. It provides a detailed view of the company's financial leverage, indicating the reliance on borrowed capital. A higher debt ratio signifies a more substantial debt load, potentially increasing financial vulnerability and affecting the company's long-term stability.

Debt Ratio = Total Debt / Total Assets

Equity Ratio

The Equity Ratio gauges the percentage of a company's assets financed by equity. It sheds light on the company's financial health and its ability to absorb losses.

Equity Ratio = Shareholders' Equity / (Total Assets - Intangible Assets)

Interest Coverage Ratio

The Interest Coverage Ratio measures a company's ability to meet its interest obligations using its operating profits. It provides insights into the company's capacity to handle interest expenses.

Interest Coverage Ratio = EBIT / Interest Expense

Price-to-Earnings Ratio (P/E Ratio)

This ratio is a valuation metric that quantifies the relationship between a company's market price per share and its earnings per share (EPS). This ratio serves as a key indicator of investor sentiment and expectations regarding a company's future earnings growth. Investors use the P/E ratio to assess the perceived risk and potential return associated with a particular stock.

P/E Ratio = Market Price per Share / Earnings per Share

Earnings Per Share (EPS)

This is a financial metric that measures the profitability of a company on a per-share basis. It is calculated by dividing the net income by the average number of outstanding shares. EPS is a key indicator of a company's ability to generate profits and is widely used by investors to assess the financial performance of a company over time.

EPS = Net Income / Average Outstanding Shares

Price-to-Book Ratio (P/B Ratio)

This ratio compares a company's market value per share to its book value per share, providing insights into how the market values a company's tangible assets. This ratio is particularly relevant for industries where asset values are a significant component of overall value, such as manufacturing or real estate.

P/B Ratio = Market Price per Share / Book Value per Share

Dividend Yield

This is a financial ratio that expresses the annual dividend income as a percentage of the current market price per share. It provides insight into a company's dividend distribution policies and is often considered by income-seeking investors.

Dividend Yield = Annual Dividends per Share / Market Price per Share

INTERPRETATIONS

Ratio	Interpretation (High)	Interpretation (Low)
Net Profit Margin	Efficient cost management and strong ability to convert sales into profit.	Inefficient cost control, challenges in converting sales into profit.
Gross Profit Margin	Effective pricing, efficient production processes, and ability to cover operating expenses.	Ineffective pricing, production inefficiencies, struggle to cover operating expenses.
Operating Profit Margin	Robust operational performance, strong core business efficiency.	Weak operational efficiency, challenges in core business activities.

Return on Assets (ROA)	Efficient asset utilisation, effective management of resources.	Inefficient use of assets, challenges in generating profit from resources.
Return on Equity (ROE)	Adept use of equity capital to generate returns for investors.	Ineffective use of equity capital struggles in generating returns for investors.
Return on Investment (ROI)	Successful investment generating a favourable return.	Unsuccessful investment with a lower return relative to the cost.
EBIT Margin	Operational efficiency and profitability in core activities.	Operational challenges, inefficiencies in core business operations.
EBITDA Margin	Strong cash operating profitability and efficient cash generation.	Cash flow challenges, inefficiencies in generating cash from operations.
Profit Margin on Sales	Effective cost management and sagacious pricing strategies.	Ineffective cost control, pricing challenges, struggles in generating profit.
Debt-to-Equity Ratio	Indicates higher financial risk, potential for higher returns but increased vulnerability.	Suggests a more conservative financial structure with lower risk.
Debt Ratio	Indicates a larger reliance on debt, higher financial risk.	Suggests a conservative capital structure, lower financial risk.
Equity Ratio	Signifies a financially stable position, better ability to absorb losses.	May indicate higher financial risk.
Interest Coverage Ratio	Signifies a comfortable ability to cover interest costs.	Indicates potential challenges in meeting interest payments.

P/E Ratio	Expectations for future earnings growth.	Potential undervaluation or lower growth expectations.
Earnings Per Share (EPS)	Positive indicator of profitability and growth.	Potential concerns about profitability and growth.
P/B Ratio	Market values the company higher than its book value.	Suggests undervaluation relative to its book value.
Dividend Yield	Attracts income-seeking investors.	May indicate a focus on reinvestment for growth.

HORIZONTAL ANALYSIS:

Horizontal analysis, commonly known as trend analysis, serves as a pivotal tool in evaluating a company's financial trajectory over consecutive periods. It allows stakeholders to discern patterns, trends, and fluctuations in key financial metrics, providing a temporal context to financial performance. This method is instrumental in identifying both positive and negative shifts in a company's fiscal landscape. Let's delve into a more detailed exploration of horizontal analysis.

Consider a fictional company, Company X, and its revenue over a three-year span:

- Year 1: $1,000,000
- Year 2: $1,200,000 (+20%)
- Year 3: $900,000 (-25%)

The upward surge of 20% in Year 2 indicates a commendable growth trajectory. This positive trend might be attributed to increased sales, improved operational efficiency, or successful market strategies. However, the subsequent decline of 25% in Year 3 raises concerns and prompts a closer examination. Questions arise: What led to this downturn? Was it a result of market dynamics, internal operational challenges, or external economic factors?

Horizontal analysis, by spotlighting these numerical fluctuations, acts as a financial detective, guiding stakeholders to investigate the underlying reasons for shifts in performance. It is not merely about crunching numbers but about deciphering the story behind the numbers – understanding the dynamics that contributed to the highs and lows. This analysis is invaluable for informed decision-making, strategic planning, and identifying areas that warrant corrective action.

It is essential to conduct horizontal analysis across multiple financial statements, including income statements, balance sheets, and cash flow statements. Examining trends in revenue, expenses, net income, and other key metrics provides a comprehensive overview of a company's financial health and operational efficiency.

VERTICAL ANALYSIS:

Complementing horizontal analysis, vertical analysis, or common-size analysis, provides a detailed breakdown of a company's financial statements, expressing each line item as a percentage of a base item, typically total revenue or total assets.

Continuing our exploration, let's look at the vertical analysis of Company X's income statement in Year 2:

- Total Revenue: $1,200,000
- Cost of Goods Sold (COGS): $600,000 (50% of Revenue)
- Gross Profit: $600,000 (50% of Revenue)
- Operating Expenses: $300,000 (25% of Revenue)
- Net Income: $300,000 (25% of Revenue)

Vertical analysis dissects the income statement, revealing the proportion of each expense category relative to total revenue. In this example, it becomes evident that COGS accounts for 50% of revenue, while operating expenses constitute 25%. This detailed breakdown aids in understanding the cost structure and profitability margins.

However, to truly grasp the implications of these percentages, it is crucial to introduce industry benchmarks. Industry benchmarks serve as benchmarks for comparison, offering a standard against which a company's financial ratios can be assessed. If, for instance, the industry average for COGS (Cost of Goods Sold) is 40%, Company X's 50% raises questions about the efficiency of its production processes or potential challenges in the supply chain.

Similarly, the comparison of operating expenses as a percentage of revenue with industry averages provides a gauge of the company's operational efficiency. If the industry norm is 20%, and Company X allocates 25%, it suggests a need for a closer look at overhead costs and operational management.

CASH FLOW

Cash flow analysis is an important component of financial assessment, playing a pivotal role in deciphering a company's financial health and strategic viability. At its core lies free cash flow (FCF), an indicator that outlines the cash available for distribution, debt management, and strategic investments.

For a company, positive FCF signifies not just profitability but the ability to generate surplus cash from core operations, providing a robust financial cushion for navigating challenges, funding growth initiatives, and returning value to stakeholders. This becomes particularly critical during economic downturns or periods of volatility, where the capacity to generate cash internally becomes a lifeline.

While net income is subject to accounting conventions and non-cash items, free cash flow offers a more tangible representation of a company's profitability and sustainability. Companies with positive and growing FCF signal financial strength, operational efficiency, and potential shareholder returns.

QUALITY OF EARNINGS

Evaluating the quality of earnings is a meticulous process in financial analysis, shedding light on the sustainability and reliability of a company's reported profits. One red flag indicating potentially lower earnings quality is aggressive revenue recognition. This occurs when companies recognise revenue prematurely or use overly optimistic estimates, artificially inflating reported earnings. Investors must closely scrutinise the consistency of revenue recognition practices, comparing them to industry standards for an accurate assessment.

One-time charges and exceptional items significantly impact earnings quality. While legitimate in certain circumstances, their frequent occurrence raises concerns about earnings sustainability. Companies may use these to manage expectations or offset operational challenges, necessitating careful assessment. Distinguishing between one-time events and recurring expenses is crucial for understanding a company's core profitability.

Exceptional items, strategically employed, can mask operational weaknesses. For instance, a company facing declining sales might report a one-time gain from asset sales, creating a temporary earnings boost. Investors must critically evaluate the nature and frequency of these items to avoid misinterpreting a company's financial health.

Aggressive revenue recognition, wherein revenue is recognised before realisation, is concerning, especially for long-term contracts. Front-loading revenue recognition can mislead investors, portraying the company as more financially robust than reality. This practice also distorts financial ratios, impacting analyses of liquidity and operational efficiency.

One-time charges and exceptional items add complexity to earnings analysis. Legitimate one-time charges, like those from restructuring, are recognised, but a consistent pattern may indicate a lack of stability or an effort to manage earnings. Evaluating the impact of these charges on earnings quality requires an understanding of their nature and frequency. For instance, a one-time gain from asset sales may temporarily boost earnings, prompting investors to assess whether it stems from strategic sales or indicates a deeper issue.

DERIVATIVES (F&O)

Derivatives are financial instruments whose value is derived from underlying assets like stocks, bonds, commodities, currencies, or interest rates. These instruments derive their value from fluctuations in the prices of the underlying assets.

The historical roots of derivatives trace back to ancient civilisations, where informal agreements were made to shield farmers and merchants from unpredictable price fluctuations of goods. The formalisation of derivatives commenced in the 19th century with the establishment of organised futures exchanges. Notably, the Chicago Board of Trade (CBOT), inaugurated in 1848, played a pivotal role in providing a centralised platform for trading standardised futures contracts, aimed at mitigating risks associated with volatile commodity prices.

There are mainly four different derivatives, namely:

- Futures
- Options
- Forwards
- Swaps

We will be discussing only two of those: Futures and Options.

OPTIONS

An option is defined as "a contract which conveys to its owner, the holder, the right, but not the obligation, to buy or sell a specific quantity of an underlying asset or instrument at a specified strike price on or before a specified date, depending on the style of the option."

A call option is a financial derivative that grants the holder the right, though not the obligation, to purchase a specified quantity of an underlying asset at a predetermined price, known as the strike price, within a set timeframe, typically until the expiration date (this varies depending on American or European options). This financial instrument is used in various markets, including stocks, commodities, indices, and other securities.

The underlying asset serves as the foundation for a call option, determining what exactly the option holder has the right to buy. This asset can span a spectrum, ranging from individual stocks to broader indices or commodities. The versatility of call options lies in their applicability across diverse financial instruments.

The strike price is the designated price at which the option holder can buy the underlying asset if they choose to exercise the option. This price is predetermined and agreed upon when the call option is initiated. The relationship between the strike price and the current market price of the underlying asset influences the profitability of the option.

The expiration date imposes a time constraint on call options. It signifies the deadline by which the option must be exercised if the holder wishes to buy the underlying asset. Beyond this date, the option becomes null and void. This time element introduces a crucial aspect of decision-making for option holders, as the timing of exercising the option can significantly impact its profitability.

The premium is the cost associated with obtaining a call option. It represents the price paid by the option buyer to the option seller for the right to buy the underlying asset. The premium is influenced by various factors, including the volatility of the underlying asset, the time remaining until expiration, and prevailing market conditions. It essentially reflects the risk and potential reward associated with the option.

There are two primary players: the call holder (buyer) and the call writer (seller). The call holder, driven by the anticipation of a future price increase in the underlying asset, acquires the call option. This individual gains the right to buy the asset at the strike price, aiming to profit from a favourable market movement.

On the flip side, the call writer is the one who sells the call option. This investor assumes the obligation to sell the underlying asset if the call holder decides to exercise the option. The call writer typically receives the premium as compensation for taking on this obligation. This role involves a different risk-reward dynamic compared to that of the call holder.

And vice versa for put options.

Note: The only difference between American and European options is that American options can be exercised at any time before or on the expiration date. On the contrary, European options can only be exercised on the expiry date.

In-the-Money (ITM) Options:

An option is considered in-the-money when the current market price of the underlying asset is favourable for the option holder's position. For call options, this means the market price is higher than the strike price, while for put options, it indicates the market price is lower than the strike price. In simpler terms, an in-the-money call option has intrinsic value because the holder could profit by exercising the option and purchasing the underlying asset at a price lower than its current market value. Similarly, an in-the-money put option has intrinsic value as the holder could sell the underlying asset at a price higher than its current market value by exercising the option.

The intrinsic value of an in-the-money option provides a cushion against potential losses and contributes significantly to the option's overall premium. Traders and investors often view in-the-money options as having a higher likelihood of being profitable, and the degree to which an option is in-the-money influences its premium.

Out-of-the-Money (OTM) Options:

Conversely, an option is deemed out-of-the-money when the current market price of the underlying asset is not conducive to the option holder's position. For call options, this means the market price is lower than the strike price, while for put options, it indicates the market price is higher than the strike price. In such cases, exercising the option would result in a loss for the holder.

Out-of-the-money options lack intrinsic value, as there is no immediate financial advantage to exercising them. Instead, the premium of out-of-the-money options is essentially composed of time value and volatility expectations. Traders and investors might choose out-of-the-money options for speculative purposes, hoping that market conditions will move in their favour before the option expires. However, these options carry a higher risk, as the market must make a substantial move to bring the option into profitability.

Sample Options Table (Nifty 50 – Indian Stock Market Index):

BID QTY	BID	ASK	ASK QTY	STRIKE	BID QTY	BID	ASK
150	628.90	631.45	50	21,150.00	5,550	4.05	4.10
50	580.05	581.65	100	21,200.00	9,350	4.90	4.95
100	530.95	532.95	50	21,250.00	7,800	6.10	6.15
100	482.85	483.95	100	21,300.00	10,550	7.90	7.95
700	435.85	436.95	800	21,350.00	12,000	10.30	10.35
200	389.15	389.95	50	21,400.00	11,100	13.70	13.75
850	343.85	344.75	100	21,450.00	13,350	18.30	18.40
50	300.35	301.05	2,000	21,500.00	4,650	24.55	24.60
400	258.80	259.50	1,550	21,550.00	3,750	32.50	32.60
50	219.25	219.55	650	21,600.00	1,850	42.95	43.00
300	183.15	183.50	850	21,650.00	650	56.55	56.65
100	149.60	149.85	1,000	21,700.00	150	73.75	73.90
100	120.30	120.50	550	21,750.00	1,450	93.90	94.10
250	94.35	94.45	350	21,800.00	700	118.00	118.25
3,150	72.00	72.10	50	21,850.00	950	145.65	145.90
1,650	54.05	54.20	1,950	21,900.00	300	177.70	177.85
2,450	40.25	40.35	400	21,950.00	100	213.45	213.95
50	29.55	29.60	6,050	22,000.00	650	252.70	253.10
6,250	21.55	21.65	2,850	22,050.00	50	294.75	295.35
5,550	15.45	15.55	13,900	22,100.00	150	338.65	339.50
8,300	11.15	11.20	4,950	22,150.00	700	384.25	385.20
1,150	8.20	8.25	21,750	22,200.00	700	431.35	432.50

The yellow-colour highlighted part is the strike price. The shaded part of the table signifies the in-the-money call or put option.

IMPLIED VOLATILITY & IV CRUSH:

Implied volatility is a metric in options trading, embodying the market's collective foresight on forthcoming price movements of an underlying asset. Unlike historical volatility, which assesses past price changes, implied volatility is forward-looking, deduced from option pricing dynamics. Computed using advanced models like Black-Scholes or Binomial, it factors in current option and strike prices, time to expiration, interest rates, and the underlying asset's present market value.

Its significance lies in influencing options pricing—implied volatility surges lift option premiums, reflecting heightened market risk, while low levels suggest a normal market. As a pivotal contrarian indicator, extreme implied volatility signals traders to reevaluate positions, presenting potential buying opportunities amid distress or indicating market complacency.

Implied volatility is prominent ahead of significant events, acting as a real-time gauge for market expectations. Traders adjust strategies based on shifts in implied volatility, utilising elevated levels for premium selling strategies and low levels for anticipating future price swings through buying options.

The term "IV Crush" refers to a significant and rapid decline in the implied volatility (IV) of an option, leading to a subsequent reduction in the option's premium. Implied volatility is a measure of the market's expectations for future price fluctuations of the underlying asset, and it plays a crucial role in determining option prices. IV Crush often occurs after a significant event such as an earnings announcement, product launch, or other market-moving news, where there is a heightened anticipation of price movement.

When these events transpire, options prices tend to reflect an elevated level of implied volatility as traders and investors anticipate substantial market swings. However, once the event has passed and the uncertainty dissipates, the need for the higher implied volatility diminishes. Consequently, the option premium, which was inflated due to the anticipated volatility, experiences a rapid decline, causing the IV Crush.

Traders who hold options positions, particularly those employing strategies that benefit from high volatility, such as long straddles or strangles (we will discuss more about such strategies soon), are particularly susceptible to IV Crush. Such traders anticipate that the market will move significantly, and they position themselves to profit from the increased option prices resulting from higher implied volatility. However, if the expected price movement does not materialise or is less pronounced than anticipated, the implied volatility contracts, leading to a decrease in the options' values.

IV Crush can catch traders off guard, as it often occurs immediately after the event when volatility expectations rapidly deflate. The impact of IV Crush is most pronounced on out-of-the-money options, as their premiums are more heavily influenced by implied volatility.

Options Strategies

Covered Call

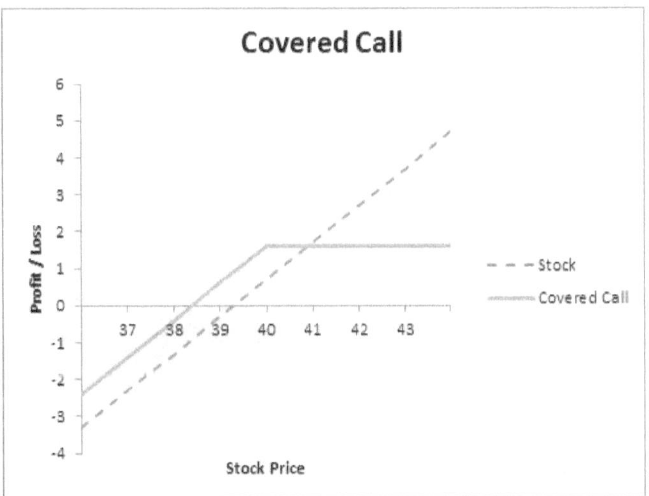

A covered call strategy involves owning the underlying stock and concurrently selling a call option against it, making it a popular approach for income generation. In this strategy, investors aim to capitalise on the premium received from selling the call option, providing an additional income stream while maintaining a long position in the underlying asset, typically stocks. The call option sold grants another investor the right to buy the stock at a predetermined price, known as the strike price, within a specified time frame. This strategy is particularly effective in a neutral to slightly bullish market environment. By selling call options, investors can enhance their overall return on investment, especially when dealing with stable stocks exhibiting limited short-term upside potential. The covered call approach is commonly adopted by income-oriented investors and those looking to gradually exit a position or generate income from a portfolio of long-term holdings. However, like any investment strategy, covered calls come with risks. The primary risk is the potential opportunity cost if the underlying stock experiences significant price appreciation, as gains are capped at the strike price. Additionally, the premium received may not fully offset potential losses if the stock experiences a substantial decline. Careful consideration of market outlook, risk tolerance, and investment objectives is crucial before implementing a covered call strategy, ensuring alignment with overall financial goals.

Protective Put

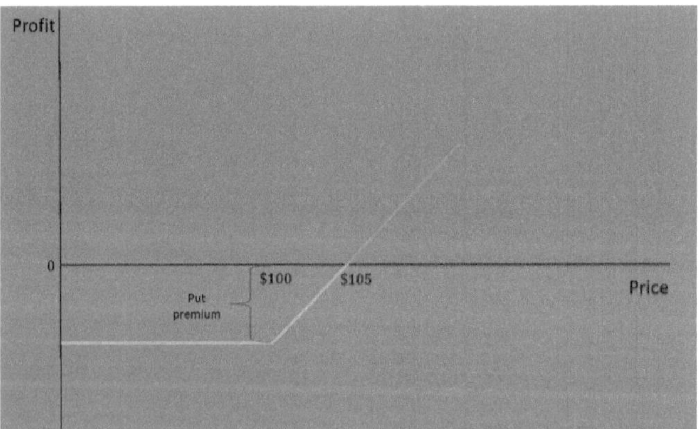

A Protective Put, commonly known as a Married Put, is an options trading strategy designed to provide investors with downside protection for an underlying stock position. This strategy involves purchasing a put option for each unit of the underlying stock held, thereby limiting the potential losses associated with a decline in the stock's price. The primary objective of the Protective Put strategy is to mitigate risk and safeguard an investor's portfolio against adverse market movements. By owning both the underlying stock and a put option, the investor has the right to sell the stock at a predetermined price (the strike price) regardless of how far the market price falls. This limits potential losses to the difference between the stock's current market price and the put option's strike price, plus the initial cost of the put option (the premium). Protective Puts are often employed by investors who are bullish on a stock but want to protect themselves against unforeseen market downturns. It is particularly useful in volatile markets or when holding a stock through uncertain events like earnings reports or geopolitical developments. While Protective Puts provide a level of security, they come with associated costs. The investor must pay the premium for the put option, which acts as an insurance cost. This upfront expense reduces the overall profitability of the stock position. Additionally, if the stock's price remains stable or increases, the investor will have sacrificed some potential gains due to the cost of the put option.

Long Call

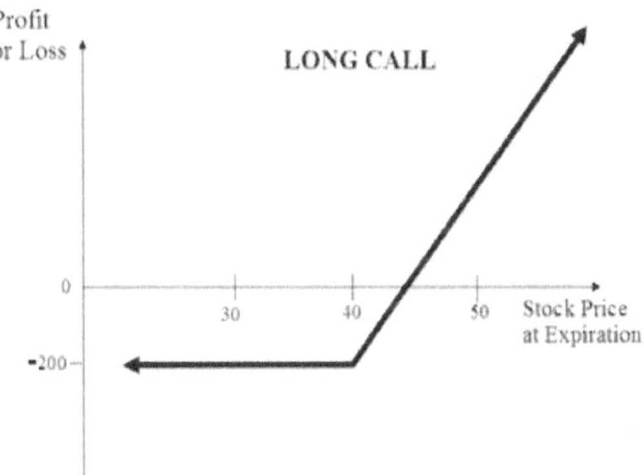

A Long Call strategy is a bullish options trading approach where an investor purchases a call option with the expectation that the price of the underlying asset will rise significantly. This strategy provides the buyer with the right, but not the obligation, to purchase the underlying asset at a predetermined strike price within a specified expiration period. The effectiveness of a Long Call lies in its potential for substantial profits if the underlying asset experiences a significant price increase. When the market price exceeds the strike price plus the premium paid for the call option, the investor can profit from the difference. This strategy is commonly employed by traders who anticipate a bullish market trend or believe that a specific stock or asset is poised for substantial growth. Long Calls are often used in scenarios where an investor wants to capitalise on short- to medium-term upward price movements. Traders may employ this strategy when anticipating positive catalysts such as earnings reports, product launches, or favourable market conditions that could drive the value of the underlying asset higher. However, it's crucial for investors to be aware of the associated risks. The primary risk with a Long Call strategy is the potential loss of the entire premium paid for the option if the anticipated price movement does not occur before the option's expiration. Additionally, time decay can erode the option's value, especially if the expected price increase takes longer to materialise.

Long Put

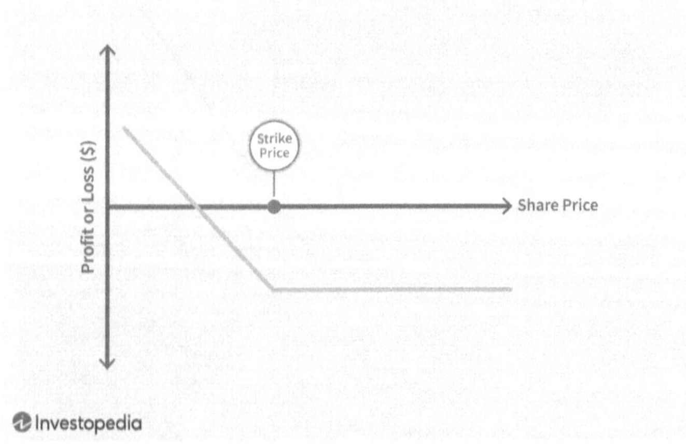

The Long Put strategy is an options trading approach employed by investors who anticipate a significant decline in the price of an underlying asset. In this strategy, an investor purchases a put option, giving them the right (but not the obligation) to sell the underlying asset at a predetermined price (strike price) within a specified time frame (expiration date). This strategy is particularly effective in bearish market conditions.

The primary motivation behind implementing a Long-Put strategy is to profit from a downward movement in the price of the underlying asset. If the asset's price falls below the strike price before the option expires, the investor can exercise the put option, selling the asset at a higher strike price and realising a profit. The potential gains are substantial, as the profit is determined by the extent of the price decline below the strike price. Long-Put strategies are commonly used by investors who believe that a particular stock or financial instrument is overvalued or poised for a significant decline. Traders may also use this strategy as a form of portfolio insurance to hedge against potential losses in a declining market. However, it's crucial to acknowledge the risks associated with the Long-Put strategy. The main risk lies in the possibility that the anticipated price decline may not occur within the specified time frame, leading to the expiration of the put option worthless. In such cases, the investor incurs a loss equal to the premium paid for the put option. Additionally, the use of options involves time decay, meaning the value of the put option diminishes as it approaches its expiration date. To mitigate this risk, investors must accurately time their trades and be mindful of the expiration period.

Straddle

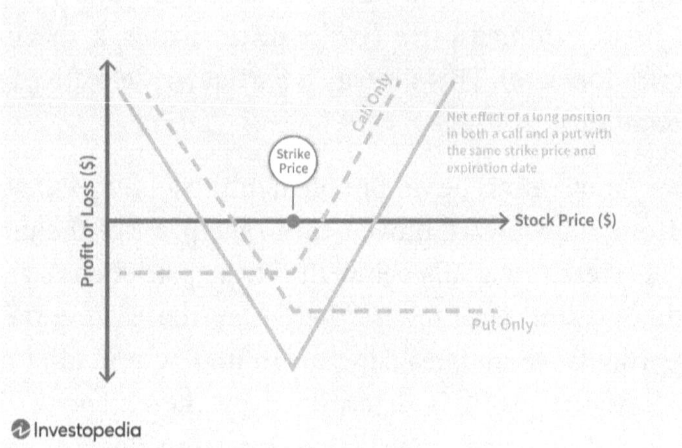

A straddle is employed by investors seeking to profit from significant price movements in an underlying asset, irrespective of the direction. This strategy involves the simultaneous purchase of a call option and a put option with the same strike price and expiration date. The premise behind a straddle is that, by holding both a bullish and bearish position, the investor is positioned to profit from substantial price swings. One key advantage of the straddle strategy is its versatility in adapting to market uncertainty. It is commonly employed in situations where traders anticipate a major price fluctuation but are uncertain about the direction of the movement. Earnings announcements, product launches, or other events that can cause substantial market reactions are typical scenarios where straddles are applied. The potential for profit in a straddle arises when the magnitude of the price movement is significant enough to offset the combined cost of both the call and put options. Traders utilising straddles aim for a high volatility environment, as increased price swings enhance the likelihood of one of the options becoming profitable. The strategy capitalises on the market's tendency to overreact to unexpected events, leading to substantial price shifts. However, it's crucial to recognise the inherent risks associated with straddles. The primary risk lies in the potential loss of the combined premiums paid for both options if the anticipated price movement does not materialise.

Strangle

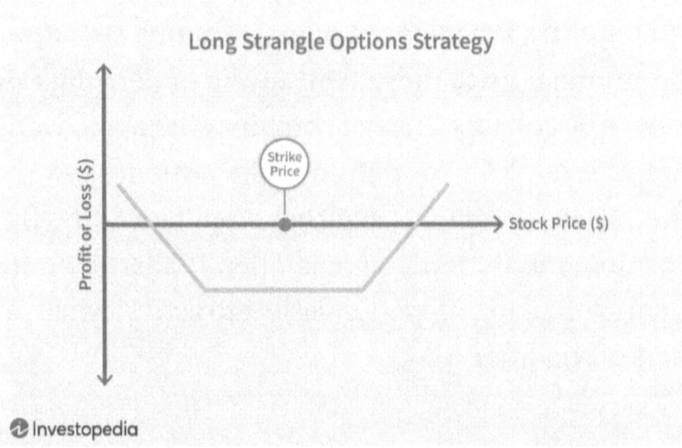

A strangle is an options trading strategy designed to profit from significant price movement in an underlying asset, regardless of the direction. This strategy involves the simultaneous purchase of an out-of-the-money call option and an out-of-the-money put option, both with the same expiration date but different strike prices. The idea behind a strangle is to capitalise on a sharp price swing while limiting the upfront cost compared to a straddle. The effectiveness of a strangle lies in the anticipation of volatility. Traders typically deploy this strategy when they expect a substantial price movement but are uncertain about the direction. Strangles are often employed during periods of heightened market uncertainty, such as around earnings announcements, product launches, or geopolitical events just as straddles. One advantage of a strangle is its lower initial cost compared to a straddle. Since both the call and put options are out of the money, their premiums are typically lower. This allows traders to establish a position with less upfront capital, making it an attractive strategy for those seeking to manage risk more efficiently. However, the primary risk associated with a strangle is the potential loss of the entire premium paid for both options, just like the straddle, if the anticipated price movement does not occur.

Butterfly Spread

The Butterfly Spread, named for its distinctive profit and loss (P&L) graph resembling a butterfly, is a nuanced options trading strategy designed to capitalise on minimal price movement in the underlying asset. Crafted with three strike prices, this strategy combines the purchase of one lower strike option, the sale of two middle strike options, and the purchase of one higher strike option, all expiring simultaneously. By creating a net debit position, the Butterfly Spread offers traders a limited risk and reward scenario, making it particularly attractive when anticipating subdued market conditions.

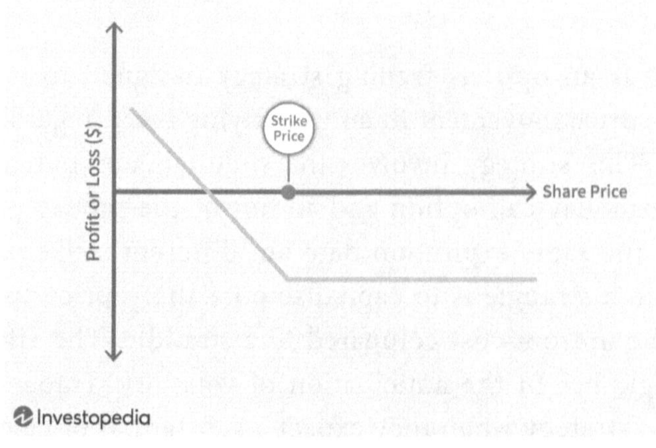

Traders often turn to the Butterfly Spread during periods of low volatility or when they expect only marginal fluctuations in the underlying asset's price. This strategy is well-suited for neutral market environments, such as consolidation phases or when an asset is trading within a narrow range. The appeal lies in its ability to provide a well-defined risk and reward structure, ensuring that the maximum loss is limited to the initial cost of establishing the position.

While the Butterfly Spread offers an attractive risk profile, it comes with its own set of considerations. Traders need to be mindful of changes in implied volatility, as significant shifts can impact the strategy's profitability. Additionally, transaction costs must be carefully weighed, as they can diminish potential profits. It is crucial for traders to adeptly navigate these factors and have a nuanced understanding of market conditions, strike selection, and the potential implications of volatility changes to effectively implement the Butterfly Spread strategy.

Iron Condor

The Iron Condor is a popular trading strategy employed by investors seeking to profit from low volatility in the underlying asset. It involves the simultaneous sale of an out-of-the-money put and an out-of-the-money call, combined with the purchase of a further out-of-the-money put and call. The result is a net credit received, as the premiums from selling the options with closer strike prices are higher than the premiums paid for the options with more distant strike prices.

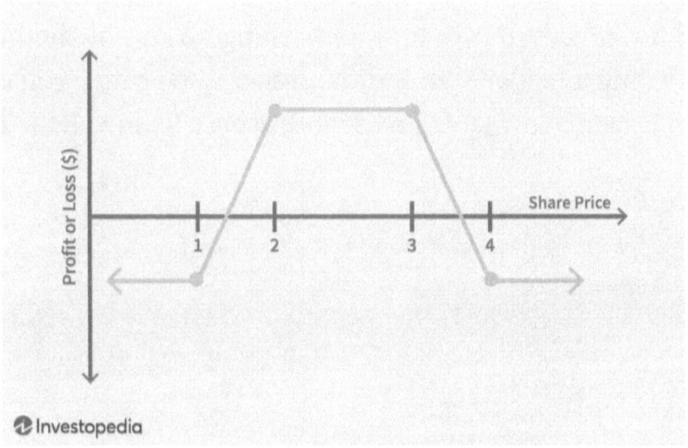

This strategy works effectively in markets with stable prices and minimal price fluctuations. Traders commonly use the Iron Condor when they anticipate that the underlying asset will remain within a specific price range until the options expire. The strategy profits from time decay and diminishing volatility, making it suitable for neutral or slightly directional market expectations.

The appeal of the Iron Condor lies in its ability to generate income with a defined risk-reward profile. The risk is limited to the difference between the strike prices of the options bought and sold, minus the net premium received. As long as the underlying asset remains within the chosen range at expiration, the options sold will expire worthless, allowing the trader to keep the premium as profit.

However, there are risks associated with the Iron Condor strategy. If the price of the underlying asset moves significantly beyond the chosen range, losses can accumulate rapidly. Traders must carefully select the width of the spread between the strike prices to balance the desire for higher premium income with an acceptable level of risk.

Collar

A Collar, also known as a Protective Collar, is an options strategy designed to protect an existing stock position from downside risk while also capping potential gains. This strategy involves simultaneously buying an out-of-the-money put option and selling an out-of-the-money call option, creating a "collar" around the stock. The primary objective of a collar is to provide downside protection, especially in volatile markets.

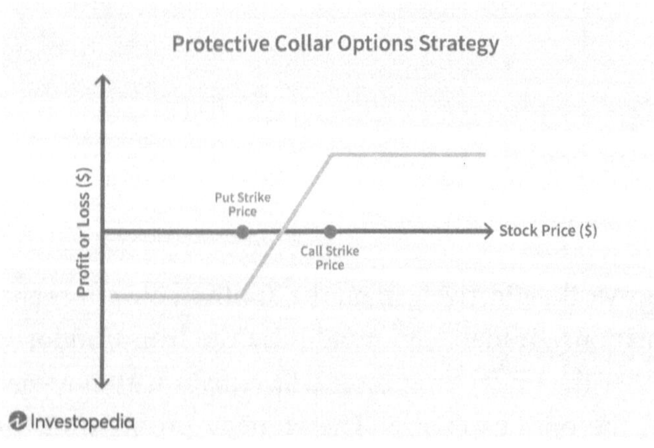

The effectiveness of a collar lies in its ability to limit the impact of adverse price movements on the underlying stock. Investors often deploy collars when they hold a substantial position in a stock and want to guard against potential losses without selling the stock outright. This strategy is particularly popular among long-term investors who wish to maintain their stock exposure while managing risk.

Collars are commonly used in situations where there is uncertainty in the market, such as ahead of important corporate events or during economic downturns. For example, an investor might implement a collar before an earnings report or during a period of increased market volatility.

One of the key features of a collar is that it offers downside protection at the cost of capping potential gains. The premium received from selling the call option partially offsets the cost of purchasing the put option. While the collar provides a floor to potential losses, it also limits the upside, as the investor commits to selling the stock at the specified strike price if it appreciates beyond a certain level.

The primary risk associated with a collar is the opportunity cost of potential gains. If the stock appreciates significantly, the investor is obligated to sell it at the predetermined strike price, missing out on profits that could have been obtained by holding the stock. Additionally, there is a cost involved in establishing the collar, as the premium paid for the put option reduces the overall return on the stock position.

Calendar Spread

A Calendar Spread, also referred to as a Time Spread, is a strategic approach that involves the simultaneous purchase and sale of options of the same type (calls or puts) with identical strike prices but different expiration dates. This tactical move capitalises on the concept of time decay, or theta (more on options Greeks), and is most effective in markets where the underlying asset's price is anticipated to remain relatively stable.

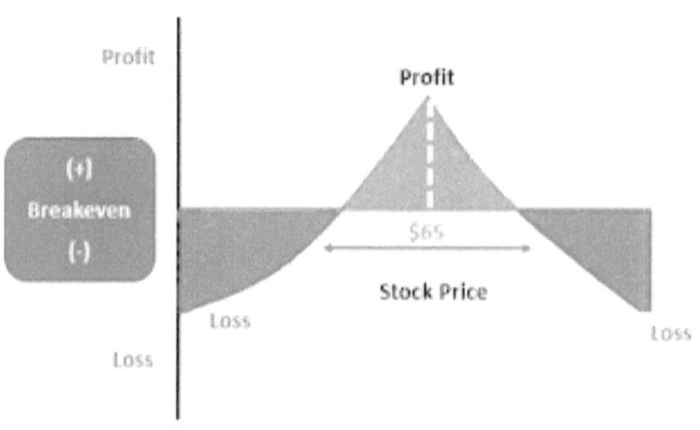

The fundamental premise behind a Calendar Spread is to leverage the differing rates of time decay between short-term and long-term options. By selling the short-term option with a closer expiration date and concurrently buying the longer-term option, traders aim to profit as the short-term option experiences a more rapid decline in value compared to the longer-term option.

Calendar Spreads find favour in neutral or mildly bullish/bearish market conditions, particularly when there is an expectation of limited price movement. This strategy is commonly employed around events such as earnings announcements, where short-term implied volatility is elevated but is anticipated to decrease in the subsequent periods.

One of the key advantages of a Calendar Spread is its relatively modest initial cost in comparison to alternative strategies. Traders can establish a position with a restrained initial investment, making it an appealing choice for those seeking a strategy with lower inherent risk. Furthermore, Calendar Spreads offer the potential for profit in scenarios where the underlying asset's price remains in proximity to the strike price.

Bull Call Spread

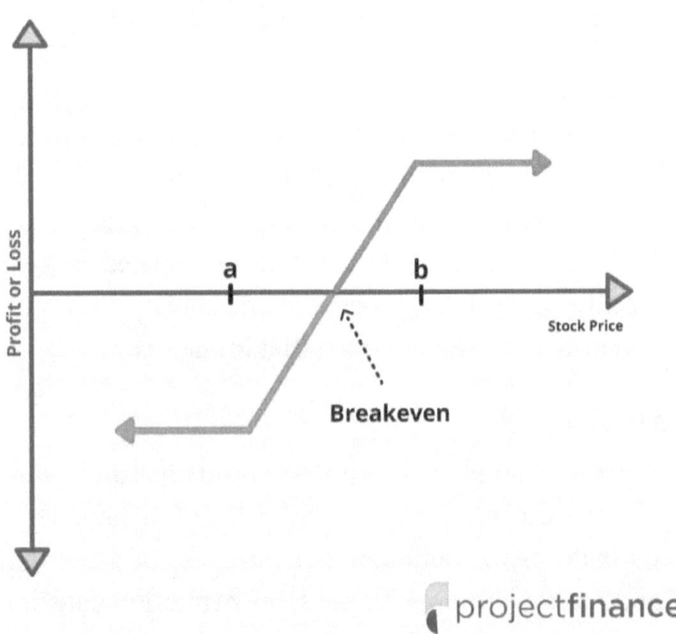

The Bull Call Spread stands as a widely utilised strategy, strategically employed by investors envisioning a moderate upward shift in the price of an underlying asset. This approach entails the purchase of a call option concurrently with the sale of another call option possessing a higher strike price, both sharing a common expiration date. The principal aim of the Bull Call Spread is to capitalise on the anticipated price upswing while concurrently alleviating the initial cost associated with the trade.

The strategy works effectively when there's a bullish outlook, but investors are also mindful of potential limitations to the upward price movement. By selling a call option with a higher strike price, the premium received helps offset the cost of buying the lower-strike call option. This results in a capped maximum loss and a capped maximum gain, offering a well-defined risk-reward profile.

Bull Call Spreads are commonly used in moderately bullish market scenarios, where investors expect the underlying asset's price to rise but wish to mitigate the impact of potential market volatility. This strategy is particularly useful when outright buying a call option might be expensive, as selling the higher-strike call helps finance the position.

One of the risks associated with the Bull Call Spread is the potential for limited profit if the underlying asset's price rises significantly beyond the higher strike price. The maximum profit is reached when the price of the underlying asset equals or exceeds the higher strike price at expiration. Additionally, there's a risk of loss if the anticipated price increase doesn't materialise, as both the purchased and sold options could expire worthless, resulting in the loss of the initial investment.

Bear Put Spread

A Bear Put Spread is employed by investors anticipating a moderate to significant downward movement in the price of an underlying asset. This strategy involves the simultaneous purchase of a put option and the sale of another put option with the same expiration date but a lower strike price. The objective is to profit from a bearish market outlook while offsetting the cost of the purchased put through the premium received from selling the lower strike put.

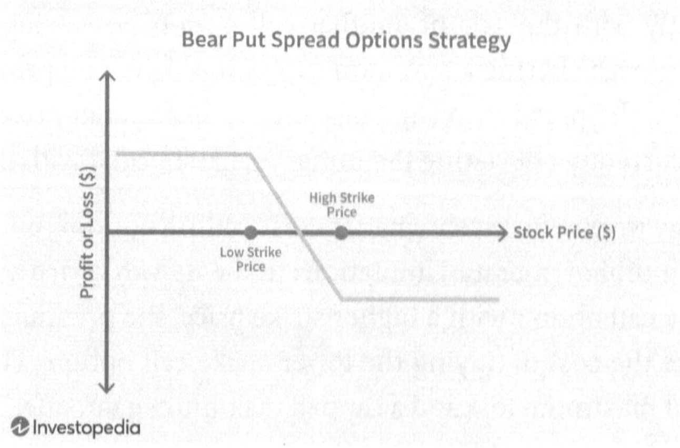

The effectiveness of a Bear Put Spread lies in its ability to provide a defined-risk approach to capitalising on bearish market expectations. By combining a long-put position with a short put position, traders can reduce the overall cost of establishing the bearish position. The strategy is particularly attractive in markets where there is a belief that the underlying asset's price will decline, but with a moderate level of uncertainty.

Bear Put Spreads are commonly used in bearish market conditions, economic downturns, or in response to specific negative news or events that may impact an individual stock or the broader market. Traders may also employ this strategy as a hedging technique to protect an existing long position in the same underlying asset.

One of the primary risks associated with a Bear Put Spread is the limited profit potential. The maximum gain is capped at the difference between the strike prices minus the net premium paid. While this limits the upside, it also makes the strategy more capital-efficient compared to simply buying a put option outright. The main risk in implementing a Bear Put Spread is the potential loss if the anticipated downward price movement does not occur.

Options Greeks

Greeks	Description	Impact	Formulae
Delta (Δ)	Measures the sensitivity of an option's price to changes in the underlying asset's price. A delta of 0.50, for example, implies that for every one-point increase in the underlying asset's price, the option's price should increase by approximately half a point.	Positive for call options, negative for put options. It indicates the expected change in the option price for a one-point change in the underlying asset's price.	$\Delta = \partial P/\partial S$ P – Call/ Put option premium S – Stock Price
Gamma (γ)	Measures the rate of change of an option's delta in response to changes in the underlying asset's price. Gamma is crucial for assessing the stability of delta. A higher gamma indicates that delta will change more rapidly in response to price changes in the underlying asset.	It indicates how much the delta will change for a one-point change in the underlying price.	$\gamma = (\partial^2) P/\partial(S^2)$ P – Call/ Put option premium S – Stock Price

Theta (Θ)	Measures the sensitivity of an option's price to the passage of time. Theta reflects the time decay of an option's premium. A theta of -0.05 means the option's price will decrease by $0.05 per day, all else being equal.	It represents the amount an option's price will decrease as time passes. Theta accelerates as the option approaches its expiration date.	$\Theta = \partial P/\partial T$ P – Call/ Put option premium T – Stock Price
Vega (v)	Measures the sensitivity of an option's price to changes in implied volatility. A Vega of 0.10, for instance, indicates that a one-point increase in implied volatility will increase the option's price by $0.10.	It reflects the change in the option price for a one-point change in implied volatility. Higher Vega values indicate greater sensitivity to volatility changes.	$v = \partial P/\partial \sigma$ P – Call/ Put option premium σ – Volatility
Rho (ρ)	Measures the sensitivity of an option's price to changes in interest rates. A rho of 0.03 suggests that for every one-point increase in the risk-free interest rate, the option's price will increase by $0.03.	It indicates how much the option price will change for a one-point change in the interest rate. Rho is more relevant for longer-term options.	$\rho = \partial P/\partial R_f$ P – Call/ Put option premium R_f – Risk Free Rate

FUTURES

We only cover futures in brief; we will not go in great depth about futures as we did in Options.

Futures contracts serve as standardised agreements between two parties, obligating one to purchase and the other to deliver a specific asset at a predetermined future date and agreed-upon price. These contracts, inherent to organised futures exchanges, are pivotal for regulated trading, efficient price discovery, and risk management. Deriving their value from underlying assets, futures contracts bridge the gap between derivatives and forward agreements.

Futures contracts fulfil a myriad of purposes, with risk management at the forefront. Businesses and individuals deploy these contracts as hedging instruments, safeguarding against adverse price movements in underlying assets. For instance, a farmer can employ a corn futures contract to secure a predetermined price for the upcoming harvest, mitigating the impact of price volatility. Speculation, a prominent purpose, involves capitalising on anticipated price movements. Speculators, spanning individual investors to institutional traders, engage in futures markets to profit from price fluctuations, enhancing liquidity and facilitating efficient price discovery.

Arbitrage, a sophisticated strategy facilitated by futures contracts, exploits price differentials between related assets or markets. Traders execute simultaneous buy and sell orders to capitalise on these divergences, contributing to market efficiency. Additionally, futures contracts offer an avenue for portfolio diversification, enabling investors to spread risk across various asset classes, from commodities to financial instruments.

The taxonomy of futures contracts encompasses financial and commodity futures, each catering to distinct underlying assets and market dynamics. Financial futures, spanning stock index futures, currency futures, and interest rate futures, provide exposure to financial instruments. Stock index futures enable speculation on future movements of indices like the S&P 500. Currency futures facilitate standardised trading linked to currency exchange rates, aiding businesses in managing currency-related risks. Interest rate futures, intricately tied to future interest rates, serve as crucial tools for mitigating risks associated with interest rate fluctuations.

Commodity futures traverse tangible assets, including agricultural, energy, and precious metals futures. Agricultural futures, such as those for wheat or soybeans, offer stability for farmers by securing prices for their produce. Energy futures, linked to commodities like oil and natural gas, manage risk within the dynamic energy sector. Precious metals futures, including gold and silver contracts, cater to investors seeking a hedge against inflation or economic uncertainty. Granularity within these categories arises through contract specifications, influencing trading strategies and risk management approaches.

Initiating a futures trade involves opening a brokerage account and depositing an initial margin, a fraction of the total contract value. This margin acts as collateral against potential losses and varies based on underlying asset volatility. Standardised expiration dates dictate when futures contracts must be settled. Traders decide whether to offset positions through an equal and opposite trade or allow contracts to proceed to settlement.

Daily settlement is pivotal, involving marking the contract's value to market at the close of each trading day. Profits or losses are realised immediately, with funds transferred between parties. Leverage, a hallmark of futures trading, magnifies both potential returns and risks. Market participants control a large contract value with a small amount of capital, but this amplification heightens the risk of significant losses. Maintenance margin requirements imposed by exchanges compel traders to maintain a minimum account balance.

Market makers play a significant role, facilitating liquidity by quoting both buy and sell prices. They narrow the bid-ask spread, fostering a more efficient and liquid market. Continuous interaction between buyers and sellers occurs through market orders and limit orders, ensuring a dynamic marketplace with real-time price discovery. The regulated and standardised mechanics of futures trading underpin transparency, liquidity, and fair market practices in this dynamic financial landscape.

DIFFERENCES BETWEEN F&O

Feature	Futures	Options
Rights and Obligations	Both parties have rights and obligations to buy/sell	The buyer has the right, but not the obligation, to buy/sell; the seller has the obligation if the buyer chooses to exercise
Profit/Loss Potential	Unlimited for both buyer and seller	Limited to the premium paid for the buyer; unlimited for the seller
Risk Level	Higher due to unlimited profit/loss potential	Limited to the premium paid for the buyer; higher for the seller
Settlement	Physical or cash settlement depending on the contract	Physical settlement for stock options, cash settlement for index options
Flexibility	Less flexible; contracts are standardised	More flexible; various strike prices and expiration dates available
Costs Involved	Initial margin, potential variation margin	Premium paid by the option buyer; no additional costs for the option seller

VOTE OF THANKS

As we wrap up our journey through the fundamentals of finance, economics, and derivatives, it's important to reflect on the key concepts we've explored. This book aimed to simplify complex topics and provide you with a solid foundation, equipping you with the knowledge and tools needed to navigate the ever-evolving world of finance.

Throughout our exploration, we've seen how finance, economics, and derivatives are intertwined, each playing a crucial role in shaping markets and influencing decisions. The practical strategies and insights provided are intended to empower you to make informed decisions, manage risks effectively, and seize opportunities with confidence.

The financial landscape is dynamic, with constant changes and challenges. However, with the foundational knowledge you've gained, you are well-prepared to adapt and thrive. Remember, continuous learning and staying informed are key to maintaining a competitive edge in this field.

As you move forward, apply these principles with diligence and an open mind. Embrace the complexity and uncertainty as opportunities for growth and innovation. Your journey in finance is just beginning, and the skills and understanding you've developed will serve as a strong base for your future endeavours.

Thank you for joining us on this journey. May your path in the world of finance be both intellectually enriching and financially rewarding.